# OBJECTIVES OF GEO-METALLURGY

SHORT Q&A

RANJIT PRASAD

*Dedicated to my Students*

# Contents

# Foreword

It givese me immense pleasure to write fore word for this book, It is a book helping the students learn basic metallurgy. i am glad that Dr. Ranjit Prasad has put effort to bring this book, which has been divided into three sections: Objective or multiple choice questions, One word or very short questions and short questions with their answers.

Mainly this book covers the questions related to Geology, geo-chemistry which are applicable and useful in understanding the metallurgical fundamentals.

This book will also help the students for the preparation of their Viva-voce exam.

This book is a valuable contribution to the fundamental studies on the basic of metallurgy specially mineral processing technology and must be made available for a wider readership, present and future, engaged in the preparation of their exam.

(Dr. S.Ranganathan)

# Preface

It is a book that aids in the students' basic metallurgical education. Three categories—objective or multiple-choice questions, one-word or extremely brief questions, and short questions with answers—are included in this book.
The majority of the topics covered in this book are those that pertain to geology and geochemistry and are pertinent to and helpful in comprehending the principles of metallurgy.
In order to prepare for their Viva-voce exam, the students will also benefit from this book.
This book is a valuable contribution to the core studies on the fundamentals of metallurgy, particularly mineral processing technology, and it must be made available to a larger readership, both current and future, who are engaged in exam preparation.

# Acknowledgements

I would want to take this opportunity to thank my B.Tech. Metallurgy students at NIT Jamshedpur who helped gather the questionnaire. My Ph.D. students Mohan Rao A, Dipali, and Suruchi in particular helped me put together the questions, and for that I am grateful. For forcing me to finish the current book, which is gratefully accepted, I must also give appreciation to Archana Thakur and my wife Mrs. Anita Prasad.

# ONE

# SEGMENT-1 OBJECTIVE Q & A

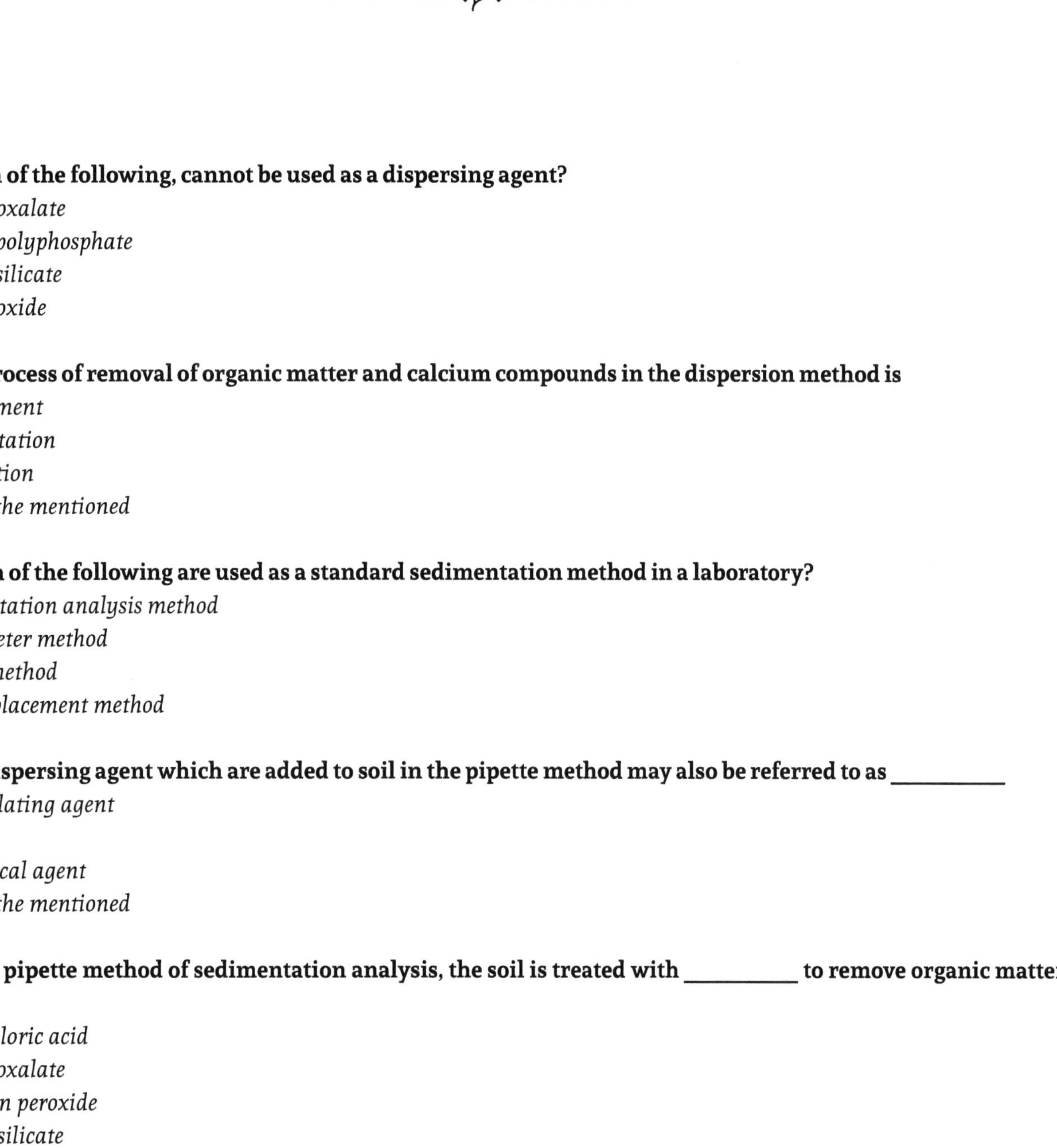

**Q. 1 Which of the following, cannot be used as a dispersing agent?**
*A. Sodium oxalate*
*B. Sodium polyphosphate*
*C. Sodium silicate*
*D. Sodium oxide*

**Q. 2 The process of removal of organic matter and calcium compounds in the dispersion method is**
*A. Pretreatment*
*B. Sedimentation*
*C. Evaporation*
*D. None of the mentioned*

**Q. 3 Which of the following are used as a standard sedimentation method in a laboratory?**
*A. Sedimentation analysis method*
*B. Hydrometer method*
*C. Pipette method*
*D. Sand replacement method*

**Q. 4 The dispersing agent which are added to soil in the pipette method may also be referred to as __________**
*A. Deflocculating agent*
*B. Calgon*
*C. Mechanical agent*
*D. None of the mentioned*

**Q. 5 In the pipette method of sedimentation analysis, the soil is treated with __________ to remove organic matter in it.**
*A. Hydrochloric acid*
*B. Sodium oxalate*
*C. Hydrogen peroxide*
*D. Sodium silicate*

**Q. 6 In the pipette method of sedimentation analysis, the soil is treated with __________ to remove organic matter in it.**
*A. Hydrochloric acid*

*B. Sodium oxalate*
*C. Hydrogen peroxide*
*D. Sodium silicate*

**Q. 7 In pipette analysis apparatus, the water outlet is present at ________**
*A. Top*
*B. Bottom*
*C. Middle*
*D. Slightly above bottom*

**Q. 8 The recommended time interval for the drainage in pipette analysis is ________**
*A. 1/2,1,2,4,8,15, and 30 min*
*B. 2,4,6,12,20 and 30 min*
*C. 1,8,16,24 min*
*D. 24,30,34,40,46 min*

**Q. 9 The volume (or) capacity of boiling tube taken in pipette method is about ________**
*A. 750 ml*
*B. 1000 ml*
*C. 500 ml*
*D. 800 ml*

**Q. 10 The dispersing agents in soil particle, may act as ________**
*A. Cementing agent*
*B. Separating agent*
*C. Soluble agent*
*D. Deflocculating agent*

**Q. 11 Flash smelting is used for the production of:**
*A. Copper*
*B. Lead*
*C. Tungsten*
*D. Aluminium*

**Q. 12 Tabling is based on the principle of:**
*A. Modification of surface tension*
*B. Difference in density*
*C. Differential initial acceleration*
*D. Differential lateral movement*

**Q. 13 The process of reducing the ore with carbon in the presence of flux is known as**
*A. Sintering*
*B. Smelting*
*C. Calcination*
*D. Roasting*

**Q. 14 Dow process is used in the extraction of:**
*A. Zinc*

*B. Aluminium*
*C. Magnesium*
*D. Lead*

**Q. 15 Which process has the objective of Precipitation of metal in aqueous solution**
*A. Leaching*
*B. Cementation*
*C. Converting*
*D. Roasting*

**Q. 16 The reagent used in the soda-lime-sinter(S-L-S) process of production of $Al_2O_3$**
*A. NaOH*
*B. $H_2SO_4$*
*C. $Na_2CO_3$*
*D. HCl*

**Q. 17 Which process is necessary for the formation of igneous rocks?**
*A. erosion*
*B. deposition*
*C. metamorphism*
*D. solidification*

**Q. 18 Electrometallurgy is a process of metal extraction which is:**
*A. Expensive but gives high purity metal*
*B. Expensive and gives low purity metal*
*C. Cheap and gives high purity metal*
*D. Cheap but gives low purity metal*

**Q. 19 Heavy media separation is based on the principle of:**
*A. Modification of surface tension*
*B. Differential lateral movement*
*C. Differential initial acceleration*
*D. Difference in density*

**Q. 20 Which one is NOT an agglomeration process?**
*A. Nodulizing*
*B. Briquetting*
*C. Roasting*
*D. Pelletizing*

**Q. 21 What is floatation separation process based on?**
*A. difference in surface properties of valuable and unwanted gangue minerals.*
*B. difference in solubility properties of valuable minerals and unwanted gangue minerals*
*C. chemical reactivity of valuable minerals and unwanted gangue minerals with certain solvents*
*D. whether the ore is sulphide or not.*

**Q. 22 Select the correct order:**
**1)selective attachment to air bubbles**

**2)physical entrapment –aggregation**

**3)entrainment**

*A. 1,2,3*

*B. 1,3,2*

*C. 3,1,2*

*D. 2,1,3*

**Q. 23 Select the correct equation:**

*A. Ys/a = Ys/w + Yw/acosα*

*B. Ys/w = Ys/a+ Yw/acosα*

*C. Yw/acosα = Ys/a + Ys/w*

*D. Yw/acosα = Ys/w*

**Q. 24 Magma that cools slowly beneath the earth's surface produces**

*A. marble.*

*B. intrusive igneous rocks.*

*C. fine-grained metamorphic rocks.*

*D. extrusive igneous rocks.*

**Q. 25 Device used to create air bubbles in the pulp: select the wrong one:**

*A. Stator*

*B. Impeller*

*C. Agitator*

*D. Launder*

**Q. 26 Contact angle is α: select the correct one**

*A. α<90 hydrophobic*

*B. α<90 hydrophilic*

*C. α>90 hydrophobic*

*D. Both (B) and (C)*

**Q. 27 Strength of froth can be estimated by:**

*A. Young's modulus*

*B. Young Dupre Equation*

*C. Young Downs Equation*

*D. Young Dupin Equation*

**Q. 28 Which of the following rocks is different from others?**

*A. marble*

*B. gypsum*

*C. sandstone*

*D. limestone*

**Q. 29 Work of adhesion =Ws/a ,Select the correct one out:**

*A. Ws/a =Yw/a + Ys/a - Ys/w*

*B. Ws/a =Yw/a + Ys/w - Ys/a*

*C. Ws/a = Ys/a + Ys/w - Yw/a*

*D. Ws/a = Ys/a + Yw/a- Ys/w*

**Q. 30 Coal and bitumen concentration cannot be done using froth floatation method:**

*A. True*
*B. False*

**Q. 31 Which of these is not responsible for the formation of igneous rock?**

*A. sediments*
*B. liquid rock*
*C. magma*
*D. lava*

**Q. 32 Entropy of the universe is**

*A. Continuously increasing*
*B. Continuously decreasing*
*C. Zero*
*D. Constant*

**Q. 33 During the formation of a chemical bond**

*A. Energy decreases*
*B. Energy increases*
*C. Energy of the system does not change*
*D. Electron-electron repulsion becomes more than the nucleus-electron attraction*

**Q. 34 According to ellingham diagram , the oxidation reaction of carbon to carbon monoxide may be used to reduce which one of the following at lowest temperature?**

*A. Al2O3*
*B. Cu2O*
*C. MgO*
*D. ZnO*

**Q. 35 Which is the purest form of Iron?**

*A. Cast iron*
*B. Ferrite iron*
*C. Wrought iron*
*D. Steel*

**Q. 36 Which one of following process is endothermic?**

*A. When conc. H2SO4 is added to the water, the water gets hot*
*B. Natural gas (CH4) is burn in Bunsen burner*
*C. Water is frozen in freezer*
*D. Water is boiled in a kettle*

**Q. 37 2CO+O2 ▸ 2CO2**
**What is the equilibrium constant Kc for the reaction?**

*A. Kc = [CO2] ^2 [CO]2 [O2]*
*B. Kc = [CO2] ^2/ [CO]^2 [O2]*
*C. Kc = [CO2]/[CO][O2] ^2*

*D. Kc = [CO2] ^2/ [CO] [O2]*

**Q. 38 A+B▸C+D ΔH0 = -10.0 kJ**
**C+D▸E ΔH0 = 15.0 kJ**
**Which one of the following reactions would have ΔH0 = -10.0 kJ**

*A. C+D →A+B*
*B. 2C+2D→2A+2B*
*C. A+B→E*
*D. 2E→2A+2B*

**Q. 39 Enthalpy of vapourization of benzene is +35.3 kJ mol–1 at its boiling point of 80°C. The entropy change in the transition of the vapour to liquid at its boiling point [in JK–1 mol–1] is ______.**

*A. –100*
*B. –441*
*C. +100*
*D. +441*

**Q. 40 The values of ΔH and ΔS of a certain reaction are – 400 kJ mol–1 and –20 kJ mol–1K–1 respectively. The temperature below which the reaction is spontaneous is**

*A. 100°K*
*B. 20°C*
*C. 20°K*
*D. 120°C*

**Q. 41 Zone refining process is used for the**

*A. Concentration of the ore*
*B. Reduction of a metal oxide*
*C. Purification of a metal*
*D. Purification of an ore*

**Q. 42 The metallurgical process in which a metal is obtained in a fused state is called**

*A. Smelting*
*B. Roasting*
*C. Calcination*
*D. Froth floatation*

**Q. 43 In van-Arkel Method, if I2 is introduced at 1700 K over imoure metal, the product is**

*A. Iodide of metal*
*B. No reaction takes place*
*C. Impurities react with iodine*
*D. None*

**Q. 44 Which of the following metals are extracted by electrolytic reduction?**

*A. Cu*
*B. Fe*
*C. AlD. Ag*

**Q. 45 Which metals cannot be obtained from electrolysis?**

*A. Ca*

*B. Mg*

*C. CrD. Al*

**Q. 46 The metal obtained by self-reduction process**

*A. Cu*

*B. Pb*

*C. Hg*

*D. All*

**Q. 47 Which of the following metals are used for reduction in metallurgy?**

*A. Al*

*B. Fe*

*C. HgD. Ag*

***Q. 48 Heating of ores with flux to remove non fusible mass is called***

*A. Roasting*

*B. Cupellation*

*C. Smelting*

*D. Poling*

**Q. 49 Which of the following metal is out as anode mud during electrolytic refining of copper?**

*A. Zn*

*B. Ag*

*C. FeD. Ni*

**Q. 50 In Electrolytic refining, the impure metal is made**

*A. Anode*

*B. Cathode*

*C. Both*

*D. None*

**Q. 51 The batch reactor has the disadvantage(s) of**

*A. high labour and handling cost*

*B. Poorer quality control of the product*

*C. considerable shutdown time to empty, clean out and refill*

*D. all of the above.*

**Q. 52 For identical feed composition and flow rate, N plug flow reactors in series with a total volume V gives the same conversion as a single**

*A. Plug flow reactor of volume V*

*B. CSTR of volume V*

*C. Plug flow reactor of volume V/N*

*D. Plug flow reactor of volume*

**Q. 53 The performance equations for constant density systems are identical for**

*A. P.F.R. and back mix reactor*
*B. P.F.R. and batch reactor*
*C. P.F.R. batch reactor and back mix reactor*
*D. Batch reactor and backmix reactor*

**Q. 54 Variables affecting the rate of homogeneous reactions are**
*A. Pressure and temperature only.*
*B. Temperature and composition only.*
*C. Pressure and composition only.*
*D. Pressure, Temperature and composition.*

***Q. 55 In a continuous flow stirred tank reactor, the composition of the exit stream***
*A. is same as that in the reactor.*
*B. is different than that in the reactor.*
*C. depends upon the flow rate of inlet stream.*
*D. None of these*

**Q. 56 A back mix reactor is**
*A. suitable for gas phase reactions.*
*B. ideal at very low conversion.*
*C. same as plug flow reactor (PFR).*
*D. same as ideal stirred tank reactor.*

**Q. 57 Sometimes, batch process is preferred over continuous process, when the product**
*A. Quality & yield cannot be achieved in continuous processes, because of long residence time.*
*B. Sales demand is fluctuating.*
*C. Both (a) & (b).*
*D. Neither (a) nor (b).*

**Q. 58 The distilled water is collected in ____________**
*A. Receiver*
*B. Adapter*
*C. Condenser*
*D. Round bottom flask*

**Q. 59 Which of the following will vaporize faster?**
*A. Aniline*
*B. Chloroform*
*C. Water*
*D. Kerosene*

**Q. 60 What is the drying temperature in the pelletising furnace for converting the green pellets into the final product?**
*A. 1250 - 1300 deg. Celsius*
*B. 200 - 800 deg. Celsius*
*C. 800 - 1500 deg. Celsius*
*D. None of the above*

**Q. 61 Why we use Pellets instead of low-grade ore as charge/feed?**
*A. It would suffer from greatly reduced productivity*
*B. It would suffer from high energy consumption rate*
*C. Ore is finely ground to separate impurities*
*D. All of the Above*

**Q. 62 What is the range of basicity of normal basic pellets?**

*A. 0.1 - 0.65*

*B. 0.1 - 0.3*

*C. 0.6 - 0.7*

*D. 0.2 - 0.5*

**Q. 63 What is the range of size of pellets after screening?**

*A. 0 – 8 mm*

*B. 8 -16 mm*

*C. 16-24 mm*

*D. None of above*

**Q. 64 What is the objective of addition of binder to the ore during pelletising?**

*A. To make the ore plastic so that it can nucleate seeds*

*B. To hold the pellet together during handling, drying and preheating*

*C. Both (A) & (B)*

*D. None of the above*

**Q. 65 What is the difference between Pelletising (P) and Sintering (S) according to sizes?**

*A. For S < 0.15 mm and P > 0.25 mm*

*B. For S > 0.15 mm and P < 0.15 mm*

*C. For S > 0.25 mm and P < 0.15 mm*

*D. None of the above*

**Q. 66 Generally, at what temperature range Sintering process is carried out?**

*A. 1300 - 1400 deg. Celsius*

*B. 800 - 1000 deg. Celsius*

*C. 1400 - 2000 deg. Celsius*

*D. None of the above*

**Q. 67 What is the Ignition Time (Approx.) during Sintering?**

*A. 0.5 – 1.0 minutes*

*B. 1.0 - 2.0 minutes*

*C. 1.5 - 2.0 minutes*

*D. 2.0 -3.5 minutes*

**Q. 68 What is the value of Basicity index for sintering?**

*A. 0.7 – 1.2*

*B. 1.2 – 1.6*

*C. 1.6 – 2.1*

*D. 0.9 – 1.8*

**Q. 69 What is the Bed Height during Sintering?**

*A. 200 – 250 mm*

*B. 275 – 315 mm*

*C. 350 - 400 mm*

*D. 400 - 450 mm*

**Q.70 As the pressure increases, rate of flow is ______**

*A. Maximum*

*B. Minimum*

*C. Constant*

*D. Same*

**Q.71 The pressure of filter aid increases the _____**

*A. Porosity*

*B. Density*

*C. Velocity*
*D. Stativity*

**Q.72 ________ is a solid material, finely divided but consisting of hard, strong particles.**

*A. Filter media*
*B. Filter aid*
*C. Filter space*
*D. Dung*

**Q.73 Filter operation should be maintained at a pressure _____ the optimum.**

*A. Maximum*
*B. Minimum*
*C. Optimum*
*D. Constant*

**Q.74 The flow rate of liquid is directly proportional to _____**

*A. Resistance*
*B. Peer bar*
*C. Pressure difference*
*D. Volume*

**Q.75 If the filtration pressure is constant, the rate of flow will _____**

*A. Increase*
*B. Diminish*
*C. Stop*
*D. Be constant*

**Q.76 When the particle has the same terminal velocity, they are said to be ___**

*A. Kinematical falling*
*B. Partially falling*
*C. Equally falling*
*D. Free falling*

**Q.77 The ratio of sizes of equally falling particles is called ___**

*A. Reflux ratio*
*B. Reduction ratio*
*C. Settling ratio*
*D. Steeling ratio*

**Q.78 In Vertical pressure filters, with high quantity feed ______ occurs.**

*A. Low filtration*
*B. High filtration*
*C. High pressure*
*D. Low pressure*

**Q.79 What is the laboratory test defined for heavy medium separation?**

*A. Float and sink test*
*B. Weight test*
*C. Bubble test*
*D. Forth test*

**Q.80 Electrolysis is usually used for metals like**

*A. Zn,Cd*
*B. Al, Ni*
*C. Ag, Sn*
*D. Si,Sb*

**Q.81 Which of the following metal(s) can be purified by zone - refining process**

*A. Si*

*B. Ge*

*C. GaD. Cu*

**Q.82 Select the correct statement(s).**

*A. rectification is done to separate metals when the difference in their vapour pressure is large.*

*B. liquation is based on difference in the melting point of metal and impurity.*

*C. Desilverisation is done by adding zinc. (Parke's process)*

*D. In electrolytic refining crude metal to be refined is made cathode.*

**Q.83 Impurities of lead in silver are removed by**

*A. Parke's process*

*B. Solvay process*

*C. Cynadie process*

*D. Amalgam process*

**Q.84 Sintering is formed...**

*A. At room temperature*

*B. Below melting point*

*C. Above boiling point*

*D. at cryogent temperature*

**Q.85 Pb which is present as impurity in silver is removed by**

*A. Parke' process*

*B. ratimaon process*

*C. Cupellation*

*D. addition of zinc in molten silver*

**Q.86 Which of the following statement is not correct?**

*A. molten lead and molten zinc are miscible*

*B. Silver is more soluble in molten zinc than in lead*

*C. Zn- Ag alloy is volatile*

*D. Zn- Ag alloy is heavier and gets solidified later than lead.*

**Q.87 The smelting zone of blast furnace is called as**

*A. Inwall*

*B. Hearth*

*C. Tigers*

*D. Bosh*

**Q.88 In which of the screens large percent of coarse materials can be separated**

*A. Grizzlies*

*B. Vibrating screens*

*C. Banana screens*

*D. Trommels*

**Q.89 Which of the following is correct?**

*A. Grizzlies capacity increases with screen angle but efficiency decreases*

*B. Grizzlies capacity decreases with screen angle but efficiency decreases*

*C. Grizzlies capacity increases with screen angle but efficiency increases*

*D. Grizzlies capacity decreases with screen angle but efficiency increases*

**Q.90 Which of the following screen gives maximum accurate sizing**

*A. Multi- deck vibrating screen*

*B. Gyratory screens*

*C. Trommels*

*D. Single deck vibrating screen*

**Q.91 One of the advantages of static grizzly**

*A. Can be movable*

*B. Gives maximum efficiency*

*C. Separates coarse particles*

*D. It requires no power*

**Q.92 Which of the following screens have high-capacity separation and also with efficiency**

*A. Trommels*

*B. Grizzlies*

*C. Gyratory screens*

*D. Vibrating screens*

**Q.93 Which of the following screens are revolving screens**

*A. Trommels*

*B. Vibrating screens*

*C. Grizzlies*

*D. Banana screens*

**Q.94 Which of the following have the highest velocity in Banana screens**

*A. Stage 1*

*B. Stage 2*

*C. Stage 3*

*D. All stages have same velocity*

**Q.95 Which of the following screens are portable and moveable?**

*A. Trommels*

*B. Gyratory screens*

*C. Vibrating screens*

*D. Grizzlies*

**Q.96 Which of the following screens have the multi-slope concept?**

*A. Banana screens*

*B. Vibrating screens*

*C. Gyratory screens*

*D. Grizzlies*

**Q.97 For what size separations industrial screening is used?**

*A. 300mm to 40μm*

*B. 300μm to 40μm*

*C. 280mm to 40μm*

*D. 280μm to 40μm*

**Q.98 A Hydro cyclone is a device to classify, separate or sort particles in a liquid suspension based on the ratio of them**

*A. centripetal force to fluid resistance.*

*B. centrifugal force to fluid resistance.*

*C. fluid resistance to centrifugal force*

*D. fluid resistance to centrifugal force*

**Q.99 In the working principal of hydrocyclone. The centrifugal force causes ____________to be 'slung' to the cone wall while _________ is kept closer to the centre.**

*A. larger particles, finer material*

*B. smaller particles, finer material*

*C. finer material, large particles*

**Q.100 The factors affecting Hydro-cyclone performance are:**

*A. diameter of vortex finder, apex and of cyclone*

*B. pressure drops inside the chamber*

*C. feed flow rate*

*D. cyclone length*

**Q.101 The vortex finder draws the water and fine material to _______ while the coarser material makes its way out the _______.**

*A. overflow,inlet*

*B. inlet,overflow*

*C. overflow, apex.*

*D. apex, overflow,.*

**Q.102 Tube projecting into central vortex of hydro-cyclone or dense medium cyclone through which the classified fines or lighter specific gravity fraction of pulp leaves the system is known as_______**

*A. Overflow*

*B. feed Inlet*

*C. vortex finder*

*D. None of these*

**Q.103 Hydro-cyclone is a**

*A. Crusher*

*B. Wet classifier*

*C. Dry classifier*

*D. Magnetic separator*

**Q.104 Classification efficiency of hydro-cyclone increases with**

*A. correct cyclone size selection*

*B. feed solids concentration and/or viscosity*

*C. by limiting water to underflow*

*D. certain geometries*

**Q.105 On increasing diameter of vortex finder, apex diameter efficiency of hydro-cyclone will**

*A. Increases*

*B. Decreases*

*C. Not depends on diameter*

*D. None of these*

**Q.106 The size for which the particles in the feed have an equal chance of going either with the overflow or underflow in Partition curve for hydro-cyclone is defined as**

*A. Cut point (d50)*

*B. fixed point*

*C. Separation point*

*D. None of these*

**Q.107 Cut-size (inversely related to solids recovery) of increases with**

*A. Cyclone diameter*

*B. Feed solids concentration and/or viscosity*

*C. low rate*

*D. Small apex or large vortex finder*

**Q.108 Ion exchange resin is**

*A. Linear*

*B. Low molecular weight*

*C. Organic polymer with porous structure*

*D. Soluble*

**Q.109 What is the dominant use of ion exchange?**

A. *Water softening with gel resin*

B. *Separation of metals*

C. *Metallurgy*

D. *Extraction of metals*

**Q.110 Ion free water coming out from exchanger is known as**

A. *Potable water*

B. *Disinfected water*

C. *Coagulated water*

D. *Demineralised water*

**Q.111 Which of the following statements is incorrect about demineralised water**

A. *It is as pure as distilled water*

B. *It is very good for use in high pressure boiler*

C. *It is fit for domestic use*

D. *It can be made either by distillation or by using cation and anion exchanger*

**Q.112 In ion exchange process, the capital cost is _____ and the operational expenses are**

A. *Low, high*

B. *Low, Low*

C. *High, High*

D. *High, low*

**Q.113 The residual hardness in ion exchange process is**

A. *0 - 2 ppm*

B. *5- 10 ppm*

C. *10-15 ppm*

D. *20- 30 ppm*

**Q.114 Which of the following phenomenon is correct about ion exchange process**

A. *Absorption*

B. *Adsorption*

C. *Sorption*

D. *All of above*

**Q.115 The exhausted anion exchange column is regenerated by passing a solution of**

A. *Dil. KOH*

B. *Conc. KOH*

C. *dil. NaOH*

D. *Conc. NaOH*

**Q.116 The exhausted cation exchange column is regenerated by passing a solution of**

A. *Dil. HCl*

B. *Conc. HCl*

C. *Dil. NaCl*

D. *Conc. NaCl*

**Q.117 Which of the following is released from cation exchange column ?**

A. *H+*

B. *Na +*

C. *K +*

D. *Ca +*

**Q.118 Which type of coal has more percentage of carbon?**

A. *Lignite*

*B. Peat*
*C. Bituminous*
*D. Anthresite*

**Q.119 What is product of bath smelting?**

*A. pig iron*
*B. Cast iron*
*C. Hot metal*
*D. steel*

**Q.120 Which type of coal is used in bath smelting?**

*A. Caking coal*
*B. Non- caking coal*
*C. Coking coal*
*D. Non - coking coal*

**Q.121 What is used for feed in bath smelting?**

*A. Sinter*
*B. Fine ore*
*C. Pellet*
*D. lump*

**Q.122 What is used to get metal from matte?**

*A. Converter*
*B. Dryer*
*C. Sintering*
*D. Palletisation*

**Q.123 Which process is more efficient to produce molten iron?**

*A. Blast furnace*
*B. Bath smelting*
*C. DRI*
*D. Electric arc furnace*

**Q.124 Which type of coal is widely use in India**

*A. Peat*
*B. Anthresite*
*C. Bituminous*
*D. Lignite*

**Q.125 Which of these process is not bath smelting process?**

*A. Corex*
*B. Hismelt*
*C. DIOS*
*D. DRI*

**Q.126 What is the product of corex process?**

*A. pig iron*
*B. liquid sponge iron*
*C. cast iron*
*D. steel*

**Q.127 How the coke is made?**

*A. By heating of coal in absence of air*
*B. by heating of coal in presence of air*
*C. by cooling*
*D. by Drying*

**Q.128 Which of the following is a characteristic/s of brittle fracture?**

*A. unstable failure process*
*B. no plastic deformation before fracture*
*C. occurs in materials with high strengths and low ductility*
*D. All of the above*

**Q.129 Ductile fracture undergoes**

*A. No plastic deformation*
*B. Little plastic deformation*
*C. Significant plastic deformation*
*D. Depends upon the material*

**Q.130 Which of the following fracture after joining can regain its original shape?**

*A. Brittle fracture*
*B. Ductile fracture*
*C. Both of the above*
*D. None of the above*

**Q.131 Tensile fracture occurs under**

*A. Low stress level*
*B. Medium stress level*
*C. High stress level*
*D. All of the above*

**Q.132 In order to understand breakage mechanism under external forces one must look into _____ loading conditions at a confining pressure**

*A. Uni-axial*
*B. Bi-axial*
*C. Tri-axial*
*D. All of the above*

**Q.133 Which of the following fracture after rejoining can't gain its original shape?**

*A. Brittle fracture*
*B. Ductile fracture*
*C. Both of the above*
*D. None of the above*

**Q.134 *A compressive shear failure occur under***

*A. Low stress level*
*B. Medium stress level*
*C. High stress level*
*D. All of the above*

**Q.135 Fracture starts from**

*A. Grain boundary*
*B. Outer surface*
*C. Internal irregularities*
*D. All of the above*

**Q.136 Brittle fracture takes place in**

*A. Fibre polymer*
*B. Ductile materials*
*C. Both of the above*
*D. None of the above*

**Q.137 Tensile strength of rocks is ________ times lower than compressive strength**

*A. one to two*

*B. 10-12 times*
*C. 50-60 times*
*D. 100-120 times*

**Q.138 The process of heating a liquid mixture to form vapours and then cooling the vapours to get pure component is called ___________**

*A. Crystallisation*
*B. Distillation*
*C. Chromatography*
*D. Sublimation*

**Q.139 Porcelain pieces are put into the distillation flask to avoid ___________**

*A. Overheating*
*B. Uniform boiling*
*C. Bumping of the solution*
*D. None of the mentioned options*

**Q.140 Which of the following will vaporize faster?**

*A. Aniline*
*B. Chloroform*
*C. Water*
*D. Kerosene*

**Q.141 The process of distillation is used for the liquids having ___________**

*A. Sufficient difference in their boiling point*
*B. Sufficient difference in their melting point*
*C. Sufficient difference in their solubility*
*D. None of the mentioned*

**Q.142 The residue in the round bottom flask is ___________**

*A. Volatile*
*B. Non volatile*
*C. None of the mentioned*
*D. Volatile & non volatile*

**Q.143 The earth's crust is the thinnest**

*A. under the mountain ranges*
*B. under continental masses*
*C. at ocean bottoms*
*D. at mid-oceanic ridges*

**Q.144 How can aniline and chloroform be separated?**

*A. Sublimation*
*B. Condensation*
*C. Distillation*
*D. Evaporation*

**Q.145 Which of the following is not separated through the distillation process?**

*A. Acetone and water*
*B. Aniline and chloroform*
*C. Impurities in Seawater*
*D. Milk and water*

**Q.146 Crushing efficiency is the ratio of**

*A. Energy absorbed by the solid to surface energy created by crushing*
*B. Energy fed to the machine to surface energy created by crushing*
*C. Surface energy created by crushing to energy absorbed by the solid*

*D. Energy absorbed by the solid to energy fed to the machine*

**Q.147 Cement clinker is reduced to fine size by**

*A. Ball mill*

*B. Roll crusher*

*C. Hammer mill*

*D. Tube mill*

**Q.148 Jigging is a technique in which particles are separated by**

*A. particle size*

*B. particle density*

*C. particle shape*

*D. None of the above*

**Q.149 Crushing of mineral particles is accomplished in a 'cage mill', when one or more alloy steel bars move in different directions. It is a type of ______ mill**

*A. Impact*

*B. roll*

*C. vibratory*

*D. None of these*

**Q.150 Which one among the following is a primary rock?**

*A. Sedimentary*

*B. Igneous*

*C. Metamorphic*

*D. None of the above*

**Q.151 Length to diameter ratio of a ball mill is**

*A. 1*

*B. 1.5*

*C. <1*

*D. >1*

**Q.152 The main size reduction operation of ultra-fine grinders is**

*A. Attrition*

*B. Impact*

*C. Cutting*

*D. Crushing*

**Q.153 Which of the following is used very large grumpy materials?**

*A. Gyratory crushers*

*B. Toothed roll crusher*

*C. Ball mill*

*D. Tube mill*

**Q.154 In case of a ball mill operating speed should be ____ the critical speed**

*A. Less than*

*B. Much more than*

*C. At least equal to*

*D. Slightly more*

**Q.155 A tube mill compared to a ball mill**

*A. Uses larger balls*

*B. Has higher length/diameter ratio*

*C. Has higher diameter/length ratio*

*D. Produces coarse product*

**Q.156 There are many types of_ surface available for industrial vibrating screens**

*A. bolt in screening*

*B. screening.*

*C. Tensioned*

*D. None of these*

**Q.157 Bolt in screening surfaces for screening duties with particles larger than around _mm frequently consist of large sheets of punched, laser cut, or plasma cut steel plate, often sandwicked with a polyurethane or rubber wear surface to maximise wear life**

*A. 70mm*

*B. 40mm*

*C. 50mm*

*D. 60mm*

**Q.158 In bolt screening surfaces these sheets are ______and are______to the screen**

*A. rigid, bolted*

*B. non rigid, unbolted*

*C. rigid, unbolted*

*D. non rigid, bolted*

**Q.159 ______sections of screens of this type are also commonly used on trommels**

*A. curved*

*B. uncurved*

*C. inclined*

*D. plane*

**Q.160 Bolt in screening surfaces are available with ____ aperture shapes and sizes**

*A. Custom-unidesigned*

*B. Custom-non designed*

*C. Custom-designed*

*D. None of these*

**Q.161 ______ screen surfaces consist of clothes that are stretched taut, either between the sides of the screen or along the length of the screen**

*A. screening surfaces*

*B. bolt in screening*

*C. tensioned*

*D. none of these*

**Q.162 In tensioned screening surfaces, increasing the wire thickness increase their ____, but decrease open area and hence capacity**

*A. strength*

*B. weakness*

*C. highly strength*

*D. weakly strength*

**Q.163 There are _____ main types of self-cleaning weave**

*A. one*

*B. two*

*C. three*

*D. four*

**Q.164 The Deccan Trap Formation was caused by**

*A. Shield eruption*

*B. Composite eruption*

*C. Caldera eruption*

*D. Flood basalt eruption*

**Q.165 ____ and ___screens are also quieter and the more flexible apertures reduce blinding compared with steel wire clothes**

*A. polyurethane and steel*

*B. steel and iron*

*C. polyurethane and rubber*

*D. none of these*

**Q.166 A soil sample may be well graded if __________**

*A. If it has the greatest number of particles of same size*

*B. Excess of certain particles*

*C. Good representation of particles of all size*

*D. None of the mentioned*

**Q.167 For coarse grained soil, the particle size D10 is sometimes called as __________**

*A. Effective size and effective diameter*

*B. Uniform diameter*

*C. All of the mentioned*

*D. None of the mentioned*

**Q.168 The shape of particle size curve, which is represented by the coefficient of curvature (Cc) is given by __________**

*A. Cc = (D30)2/D10×D40*

*B. Cc = (D40)2/D10×D30*

*C. Cc = (D30)2/D10×D60*

*D. Cc = D60/D10*

**Q.169 The coefficient of uniformity (CV) is the ratio of _________**

*A. D60 and D10*

*B. D30 and D10*

*C. D10 and D30*

*D. D10 and D30*

**Q.170 The curve situated at the right side of the particle size distribution curve is _________**

*A. Coarse-grained soil*

*B. Fine-grained soil*

*C. coarse-grained soil*

**Q.171 What is the time of settlement of coarse particles of a soil sample, of diameter 0.5? Take γ=0.905D2 and the height of the water tank as 5 m.**

*A. 11.6 seconds*

*B. 72.8 seconds*

*C. 14 seconds*

*D. 22.1 seconds*

**Q.172 A curve with a flat portion, in particle size distribution curve represent __________**

*A. Intermediate size particle are missing*

*B. Intermediate size particles are present*

*C. Smaller size particle are present*

*D. Large size particles are present*

**Q.173 The D10 represents a size, such that _________ of the particles are finer than this size.**

*A. 20%*

*B. 60%*

*C. 10%*

*D. 100%*

**Q.174 The time of settlement of the finest particle of soil sample is 15hr20min49sec. calculate the height of the water tank. Take D=0.01 mm, γ=0.905D2.**

*A. 5 m*

*B. 7 m*

*C. 12 m*

*D. 4 m*

**Q.175 The shape of the particle size curve is represented by ________**

*A. Effective size*

*B. Effective diameter*

*C. Uniform coefficient*

*D. Coefficient of curvature*

**Q.176 In order to bring initial chemical change in the ore, the process of heating of ore below its melting point is known as:**

*A. Reduction*

*B. Smelting*

*C. Calcination*

*D. Roasting*

**Q.177 The cheap and having high melting point compound used in furnace is:**

*A. PbO*

*B. Cao*

*C. HgO*

*D. ZnO*

**Q.178 In Bayer process, bauxite is digested under pressure using :**

*A. H2SO4*

*B. NH3*

*C. NaOH*

*D. HCl*

**Q.179 Blast Furnace is employed in the smelting of oxide ore with coke & flux in the metallurgy of:**

*A. Fe*

*B. Cu*

*C. Pb*

*D. All the above*

**Q.180 Roasting depends on which of the following factors?**

*A. Time*

*B. Temperature*

*C. Availability of O2*

*D. All of the above*

**Q.181 Which of the following substance can be used for drying gases:**

*A. CaCO3*

*B. NaHCO3*

*C. Na2CO3*

*D. CaO*

**Q.182 Matte contains mainly:**

*A. Cu2S & FeS*

*B. CuS & Fe2S3*

*C. Fe*

*D. Cu2S*

**Q.183 A metal obtained directly by roasting of it's sulphide ore is :**

*A. Cu*

*B. Pb*

*C. HgD. Zn*

**Q.184 In blast furnace, the highest temperature is in :**

*A. Reduction Zone*

*B. Slag Zone*

*C. Fusion Zone*

*D. Combustion Zone*

**Q.185 Heating mixture of $Cu_2O$ & $Cu_2S$ in reverberatory furnace to get metallic Cu will give:**

*A. $Cu+SO_2$*

*B. $Cu+SO_3$*

*C. $CuO+CuS$*

*D. $Cu_2SO_3$*

**Q.186 All types of coals can be converted into coke.**

*A. True*

*B. False*

**Q.187 Which coals are suitable for metallurgical purposes?**

*A. Coking*

*B. Carburized*

*C. Non-coking*

*D. Decarburized*

**Q.188 Caking coal with ______ content are used for gas manufacturers.**

*A. high volatile matter*

*B. low volatile matter*

*C. high ash content*

*D. high moisture content*

**Q.189 Select the correct statement among the given below.**

*A. All coking coals are caking but not all caking coals are coking*

*B. All caking coals are coking but not all coking coals are caking*

*C. Coking and caking are the same types of coals*

*D. All types of coals can be coked*

**Q.190 Presence of free moisture in coal during its high temperature carbonization**

*A. Reduces the coking time*

*B. Protects the volatile products from pyrolysis (cracking) in the presence of hot coke and hot oven walls*

*C. Increases the loss of fine coal dust from the ovens when charging*

*D. None of these*

**Q.191 Caking index of coal is measure of its**

*A. Abradability*

*B. Reactivity*

*C. Agglutinating (binding) properties*

*D. Porosity*

**Q.192 The advantage of firing pulverised coal in the furnace lies in the fact, that it**

*A. Permits the use of high ash content coal*

*B. Permits the use of low fusion point ash coal*

*C. Accelerates the burning rate and economic on fuel combustion*

*D. All of the above*

**Q.193 Blast furnace coke is made from coal by**

*A. Low temperature carbonisation*

*B. High temperature carbonisation*

*C. Medium temperature carbonisation*

*D. Heating the coal in an oven in presence of air*

**Q.194 Low temperature carbonisation:**

*A. Is mainly for producing the smokeless domestic coke*

*B. Is meant for the production of 'metallurgical coke'*

*C. Produces higher quantity of gas than high temperature carbonisation*

*D. Produces less quantity of tar than high temperature carbonisation*

**Q.195 Prime coking coal is always blended with medium or non-coking coal before carbonisation**

*A. To check against its excessive swelling during heating, which may exert high pressure and damage coke oven walls*

*B. Because, it alone produces unreactive coke*

*C. Both A&B*

*D. Neither A nor B*

**Q.196 Pick out the wrong statement**

*A. In a batch reactor, which is exclusively used for liquid phase reactions, temperature, pressure and composition may vary with time.*

*B. In a continuous flow reactor, both the reactants and the products flow out continuously.*

*C. In a continuous flow reactor, uniform concentration cannot be maintained throughout the vessel even in a well agitated system.*

*D. In a semi-batch reactor, one reactant is charged batchwise, while the other reactants are fed continuously.*

**Q.197 For nearly isothermal operation involving large reaction time in a liquid-phase reaction, the most suitable reactor is a which reactor?**

*A. tubular flow*

*B. stirred tank*

*C. batch*

*D. fixed bed*

**Q.198 A batch reactor is characterised by**

*A. very low conversion*

*B. variation in reactor volume*

*C. constant residence time*

*D. variation in extent of reaction and properties of the reaction mixture with time.*

**Q.199 Which of the following is a directly-fired intermittant furnace?**

*A. Tunnel kiln*

*B. Reverberatory furnance*

*C. Tower furnace*

*D. Walking beam-reheating furnace*

**Q.200 In furnaces operating at very high temperature (say...1250degree Celsius),the maximum heat transfer takes place by**

*A. Convection*

*B. Conduction*

*C. Radiation*

*D. cannot be prediction*

**Q.201 Coal gasification can be done by which of the following**

*A. Fluidized bed reactor*

*B. Electric furnances*

*C. reverberatory furnanaces*

*D. rotary kilns*

**Q.202 Which reactor can handle material with variable particle size?**

*A. Shaft*

*B. fluidized-bed reactors*

*C. rotary kilns*

*D. electric furnaces*

**Q.203 which reactor are used in cases where contact with hot oxidizing combustion gases would be harmful for the charge?**

*A. Retort*

*B. electric furnaces*

*C. Reverberatory furnaces*

*D. fluidized-bed reactors*

**Q.204 Which reactor is used in the burning of limestone?**

*A. shaft furnaces*

*B. fluidized-bed reactors*

*C. electric furnaces*

*D. retorts*

**Q.205 These furnaces are used for matte smelting and the smelting of iron and ferroalloys, as well as for the steel making.**

*A. shaft furnaces*

*B. fluidized-bed reactors*

*C. electric furnaces*

*D. retorts*

**Q.206 In case of coarse-grained materials, select the right combination of stroke length and stroke frequency: -**

*A. short & low*

*B. long & low*

*C. short & high*

*D. long & high*

**Q.207 What must be the minimum difference between the densities of heavier and lighter particles to be sorted on shaking?**

*A. 0.5*

*B. 1.5*

*C. 1*

*D. 1.25*

**Q.208 Which of the following statements is/are correct?**

*A. The major constituent mineral of granite rock is quartz.*

*B. The major constituent mineral of sandstone rock is feldspar.*

*C. The major constituent mineral of limestone rock is dolomite.*

**Q.209 Select the right combination of deck slope with size of materials. (Assume water flow amount is appropriate)**

*A. (3.5-4) °, (0.5-2) mm*

*B. (2.5-3.5) °, (0.1-0.5) mm*

*C. (2-2.5) °, (less than 0.1) mm*

*D. All*

**Q.210 In case of fine-grained materials, select the right combination of stroke length and stroke frequency:**

*A. Short & high*

*B. Long & high*

*C. Short & low*

*D. Long & low*

**Q.211 The ilmenite particles settle at the bottom of ridges in between riffles, when separated from silica in a shaking table.**

*A. True*
*B. false*

**Q.212 Select correct options.**

*A. Higher water flow rate, higher grade*
*B. Lower water flow rate, higher grade*
*C. Feed flow rate increases, grade increases*
*D. Deck tilt angle lowers, grade lowers*

**Q.213 The mass of valuable in concentration is 35 gm and mass of valuable in ore is 77 gm. Find the recovery.**

*A. 39 %*
*B. 40 %*
*C. 45 %*
*D. 20 %*

**Q.214 Calculate the grade when mass of valuable in concentrate is 25 gm and mass of concentrate is 63 gm.**

*A. 39.7 %*
*B. 41 %*
*C. 37 %*
*D. 30 %*

**Q.215 The continuous supply of soft water can be provided by having________.**

*A. storage facilities*
*B. required amount of ppm*
*C. high pressure boiler*
*D. 1 ppm*

**Q.216 Which of the following statement is incorrect about the demineralised water?**

*A. It is as pure as distilled water*
*B. It is very good for use in high pressure boilers*
*C. It is fit for domestic use*
*D. It can be made either by distillation or by using cation and anion exchangers*

**Q.217 The mineral free water is not used in __________.**

*A. Pharmaceuticals*
*B. Cosmetics*
*C. Explosives*
*D. Drinking*

**Q.218 The residual hardness after the treatment of water is about __________.**

*A. 1 ppm*
*B. Less than 1ppm*
*C. 2 ppm*
*D. Less than 2pmm*

**Q.219 In case of the zeolites, ion exchange process does not function properly because of the __________.**

*A. Turbidity*
*B. Suspended matter*
*C. Turbidity and suspended matter*
*D. Neither turbidity nor suspended matter*

**Q.220 The regeneration of acids and alkalis in ion exchange process is __________.**

*A. Cheaper*
*B. Costlier*

*C. Time taking*
*D. Hard process*

**Q.221 Ion exchange process is the clean process because it has__________.**

*A. Sludge formation*
*B. No sludge formation*
*C. Little sludge is formed*
*D. Other precipitates are formed*

**Q.222 Water softened during _________ method will be ideal in boilers.**

*A. Zeolite method*
*B. Lime soda method*
*C. Demineralization method*
*D. Permutit's process*

**Q.223 The hardness in the ion exchange process is reduced to __________.**

*A. 0-1ppm*
*B. 0-2ppm*
*C. 0-3ppm*
*D. 0-4ppm*

**Q.224 Which of these chromatography types are suitable as a "capture" step in the purification of non- tagged protein?**

*A. size exclusion chromatography (SEC).*
*B. Dialysis*
*C. ion exchange (IEX) and hydrophobic interaction (HIC).*
*D. Ammonium sulphate precipitation.*

**Q.225 Impact strength of a material is an index of its is?**

*A. Toughness*
*B. Tensile strength*
*C. Hardness*
*D. Plasticity*

**Q.226 % Of elongation during tensile test is indicative of**

*A. Ductile*
*B. Brittle*
*C. Plasticity*
*D. Hardness*

**Q.227 In stress strain curve the load at which there is considerable extension without increase in stress**

*A. Lower yield point*
*B. Fracture point*
*C. upper yield point*
*D. Elasticity limit*

**Q.228 The material in which large deformation is possible before the absolute failure or fracture?**

*A. Brittle*
*B. Elastic*
*C. Ductile*
*D. Tensile*

**Q.229 With an increase in the degree of cold working tensile strength of material?**

*A. Increase*
*B. Decrease*
*C. Remain Constant*

**Q.230 Tensile strength of a material is obtained by dividing the maximum load during the test by**

*A. area at the time fracture*
*B. Original cross sections*
*C. a and b both*
*D. minimum area of fracture*

**Q.231 For steel the UTS in shear as compared to in tension is nearly**

*A. same*
*B. Half*
*C. one third*
*D. one fourth*

**Q.232 In tensile test, the phenomenon of slow extension of the material i.e., stress increasing with the time at constant load**

*A. Creeping*
*B. Yielding*
*C. Breaking*
*D. None of these*

**Q.233 The ratio of elongation in a prismatic bar due to its own might as compared to another similar bar carrying an additive weight will be**

*A. 1:2*
*B. 1:3*
*C. 1:4*
*D. 1:2.5*

**Q.234 A non-yielding support implies that**

*A. support is frictionless*
*B. support can take any amount of reaction*
*C. Support with member firmly*
*D. The support of break is zero*

**Q.235 Which of the following does not influence filtration?**

*A. Temperature*
*B. Density*
*C. ViscosityD. pH*

**Q.236 The slurry is _______________**

*A. A suspension to be filtered*
*B. A porous membrane used to retain the solids*
*C. The solids which are present on the filter*
*D. A clear liquid passing through the filter*

**Q.237 What do you mean by filter cake?**

*A. The cake which is to be filtered*
*B. A porous membrane used to retain the solids*
*C. The solids which are present on the filter*
*D. A suspension to be filtered*

**Q.238 Which of the following process is used to separate insoluble particles from liquids?**

*A. Filtration*
*B. Extraction*
*C. Drying*
*D. Sieving*

**Q.239 Which of the following is not the application of filtration?**

*A. Sterilization of media*

*B. Removal of debris*
*C. Plasma clarification*
*D. Off-gas analysis*

**Q.240 Which of the following filtration equipment offers maximum pressure drop?**
*A. Plate and frame filter press*
*B. Pressure leaf filter press*
*C. Continuous Rotary Vacuum Filter Press*
*D. None of the mentioned*

**Q.241 Statement 1: Continuous Rotary vacuum filter press has a high labor cost.**
**Statement 2: Continuous Rotary vacuum filter press has a high clogging.**
*A. True, False*
*B. True, True*
*C. False, False*
*D. False, True*

**Q.242 If the aperture size of the filtration medium is too small, it causes high pressure drops.**
*A. True*
*B. False*

**Q.243 Which of the following process is not involved in sludge thickening?**
*A. Gravity thickening*
*B. Vacuum filter*
*C. Air flotation*
*D. Centrifugation*

**Q.244 Which of the following filtration equipment operates under continuous operation?**
*A. Plate and frame filter press*
*B. Pressure leaf filter press*
*C. Continuous Rotary Vacuum Filter Press*
*D. None of the mentioned*

**Q.245 In ellingham diagram of oxide formation vs temperature which of the following graphs has negative slope?**
*A. C * CO*
*B. Fe * Fe2O3*
*C. Mg*MgO*
*D. ALL OF THESE*

**Q.246 Aluminium is used as a reducing agent in the reduction of**
*A. Cr2O3*
*B. SnO2*
*C. ZnO*
*D. HgO*

**Q.247 Consider the following reactions at 1000*c**
*1. Zn(S) + (1/2)O2(g) * ZnO dG=-360KJ/MOLE*
*2. C(s) +(1/2)O2 * CO(g) dG=-460KJ/MOLE*
*and choose the correct statement at 1000*c*
*A. Zno is more stable than CO*
*B. Zno can be reduced to zn by C*
*C. Zno and Co are formed at equal rate*
*D. Zno cannot be reduced to zn by C*

**Q.248 Select the correct statement:**
*A. In the decomposition of an oxide into oxygen and gaseous metal, entropy increases*

*B. Decomposition of an oxide is an endothermic change*
*C. To make dG negative, temperature should be high enough so that TdS > dH*
*D. All are correct*

**Q.249 Ellingham diagram represents a graph of:**

*A. dG vs T*
*B. dG* vs T*
*C. dS vs P*
*D. dG vs P*

**Q.250 In the extraction of copper from its sulphide ore , the metal is formed by the reduction of cu2o with**

*A. FeS*
*B. CO*
*C. Cu2S*
*D. SO2*

**Q.251 In the metallurgy of alluminium**

*A. Al3+ is oxidised to al*
*B. graphite anode is oxidised to carbon monoxide and carbon dioxide*
*C. oxidation state of oxygen changes in the reaction at anode*
*D. oxidation state of oxygen changes in the overall reaction involved in the process*

**Q.252 dG* vs T plot in the ellinghams diagram slopes downward for the reaction**

*A. Mg + (1/2) O2 * MgO*
*B. 2Ag +(1/2) O2 * Ag2O*
*C. C + (1/2) O2 * CO*
*D. CO + (1/2) O2 * CO2*

**Q.253 Main function of Roasting is**

*A. Remove volatile substance*
*B. Oxidation*
*C. Reduction*
*D. Slag formation*

**Q.254 Which of the following substance can be used as drying gases?**

*A. CaCO3*
*B. Na2CO3*
*C. NaHCO3*
*D. CaO*

**Q.255 In which type of filtration subatomic pressure is used?**

*A. gravity filters*
*B. centrifugal filters*
*C. vacuum filters*
*D. pressure filters*

**Q.256 which type of anode is used in electrowinning process?**

*A. impure metal*
*B. inert*
*C. electropositive metal*
*D. electronegative metal*

**Q.257 which reaction happens during cementation process?**

*A. oxidation reaction*
*B. reduction*
*C. redox*
*D. none*

**Q.258 In which of these solid-liquid separation processes flocculants are used?**

A. *washing*

B. *filtration*

C. *thickening*

D. *settling*

**Q.259 Which type of leaching is also known as solution leaching?**

A. *tank leaching*

B. *in –situ leaching*

C. *heap leaching*

**Q.260 Which of the type of leaching is also known as agitation leaching?**

A. *heap leaching*

B. *tank leaching*

C. *vat leaching*

**Q.261 In which type of leaching holes are drilled in the ore deposits?**

A. *autoclave leaching*

B. *vat leaching*

C. *in-situ leaching*

**Q.262 Which type of Flash Smelting Process is?**

A. *Hydrometallurgical Process.*

B. *Pyrometallurgical Process.*

C. *Electrometallurgical Process.*

D. *None of these.*

**Q.263 Flash Smelting Process is used for which type of Ore?**

A. *Oxide Ore.*

B. *Carbonate Ore.*

C. *Halide Ore.*

D. *Sulphide Ore.*

**Q.264 Flash Smelting Process (Outukumpu) is mainly used to extract which Metal?**

A. *Copper.*

B. *Zinc.*

C. *Iron.*

D. *Nickel.*

**Q.265 Flash Smelting Process (INCO) is mainly used to extract which Metal?**

A. *Iron.*

B. *Magnesium.*

C. *Nickel.*

D. *Chromium.*

**Q.266 Flash Smelting is a --------- process.**

A. *Highly Endothermic.*

B. *Highly Exothermic.*

C. *Endothermic.*

D. *Exothermic.*

**Q.267 What is MATTE?**

A. *Metal Sulphide.*

B. *Metal Oxide.*

C. *Metal Hydroxide.*

D. *Metal carbonate.*

**Q.268 Which is the ore of copper?**

*A. Covellite.*

*B. Bornite.*

*C. Sphalerite.*

*D. All of the above.*

**Q.269 What is temperature of Outukumpu Flash Furnace during extraction of Copper?**

*A. Above 3000K.*

*B. Below 1000K.*

*C. Above 1500K.*

*D. Below 2000K.*

**Q.270 Which State of India produces the most Copper?**

*A. Uttar Pradesh.*

*B. Madhya Pradesh.*

*C. Maharashtra.*

*D. Orissa.*

**Q.271 Which Country Produces the most Copper?**

*A. India*

*B. Australia.*

*C. Russia.*

*D. Chile.*

**Q.272 Which of the following properties is not associated with refractory metals?**

*A. High fusion temperature*

*B. High heat resistance*

*C. Good Corrosion resistance*

*D. High thermal coefficient of expansion*

**Q.273 What is the fusion temperature of aluminum silica?**

*A. 1780oC*

*B. 1900oC*

*C. 2050oC*

*D. 2800oC*

**Q.274 Which of the following is an example of a neutral refractory?**

*A. Dolomite*

*B. Magnesia*

*C. Silica*

*D. Chromite*

**Q.275 What is the fusion temperature of Magnesia?**

*A. 1700oC*

*B. 2180oC*

*C. 2800oC*

*D. 3500oC*

**Q.276 Silica refractories are also known as ______ refractories.**

*A. Acid*

*B. Basic*

*C. Neutral*

*D. Magnesia*

**Q.277 What kind of refractory can bauxite be grouped as?**

*A. Acid refractory*

*B. Basic refractory*

*C. Neutral refractory*

*D. Silica refractory*

**Q.278 How much of alumina in weight percent is added to silica refractories?**

*A. 0.2 – 1.0*

*B. 1.1 – 1.5*

*C. 1.6 – 1.8*

*D. > 2.0*

**Q.279 Mullite is an example of ______ refractory.**

*A. Acid*

*B. Basic*

*C. Neutral*

*D. Special*

**Q.280 How much silica do silica refractories usually contain?**

*A. 95 – 97%*

*B. 0.2 – 1.0%*

*C. 1.8 – 3.5%*

*D. 0.3 – 0.9%*

**Q.281 Firebrick is an important raw material of refractory metals, which is made from ______**

*A. Brick*

*B. Concrete*

*C. Fireclay*

*D. Wood*

**Q.282 Layers dipping at angles up to 45° may be called __________**

*A. Moderately inclined strata*

*B. Steeply inclined strata*

*C. Half inclined strata*

*D. Semi-inclined strata*

**Q.283 Which of the following brings sea erosion?**

*A. Hydraulic action*

*B. Abrasion*

*C. Corrosion*

*D. All of the above*

**Q.284 Which of the following action leads to the formation of sea cliffs?**

*A. Sawing action*

*B. Chopping action*

*C. Both a and b*

*D. None of these*

**Q.285 Coastal zone occupies________**

*A. 15%*

*B. 25%*

*C. Less than 15%*

*D. Less than 25%*

**Q.286 Which of the following are littoral deposits?**

*A. Shore of the sea*

*B. Shore of the river*

*C. Section between low and high tide*

*D. None of these*

**Q.287 ________ activity can lead to the formation of hydrogen sulphide.**

*A. Fungus*

*B. Bacterial*

*C. Virus*

*D. All of the above*

**Q.288 Up to which distance, the great barrier reef extends laterally?**

*A. Nearly 1000 km*

*B. Nearly 1500 km*

*C. Nearly 2000 km*

*D. Nearly 2500 km*

**Q.289 Which of the following are not Hard Solution for coastal protection?**

*A. Artificial beach nourishment*

*B. Revetments*

*C. See walls*

*D. None of these*

**Q.290 Which of the following points related to Groynes?**

*A. May cause down-drift erosion*

*B. Normally constructed in series, perpendicular to the short line*

*C. Traps sediments by interrupting or reducing longshore drift*

*D. All of the above*

**Q.291 Why is the protection against rising sea levels in the 21st century crucial?**

*A. Sea level decreases*

*B. Sea level rise accelerates*

*C. Changes in sea level damage*

*D. All of the above*

**Q.292 How much of the Earth's water is stored in underground aquifers?**

*A. less than 1%*

*B. about 5%*

*C. about 10%*

*D. about 20%*

**Q.293 What is the process by which water enters the small pore spaces between particles in soil or rocks?**

*A. Transpiration*

*B. Infiltration*

*C. Precipitation*

*D. Sublimation*

**Q.294 Which of the following is not a disadvantage, in using the pipette method for sedimentation analysis?**

*A. The apparatus is very simple*

*B. Requires very accurate weight*

*C. It requires more time*

*D. The method of process is simple*

**Q.295 Which of the following involves vibrations?**

*A. Ball mill*

*B. Roll mill*

*C. Grizzly screen*

*D. Hammer mill*

**Q.296 Pick the rock considered as soft rocks for tunnelling.**

*A. Granite*

*B. Gabbro*

*C. Basalt*

*D. Shale*

**Q.297 What are the types of soil samples?**

*A. Disturbed soil sample, undisturbed soil sample*

*B. low density soil sample, high density soil sample*

**Q.298 How many of the following are not correct for lead extractions**

*A. Principle ore is Galena (PbS)*

*B. ore is concentrated by magnetic separation*

*C. PbO is reduced by coke in blast furnace*

*D. The metal produced from blast furnace is called lead bullion.*

*E. Pb also undergoes self-reduction*

*F. Galena contains impurity as ZnS, FeS2, Cu2S, Ag, Au etc*

**Q.299 The coefficient of uniformity (CV) is the ratio of ________**

*A. D60 and D10*

*B. D30 and D10*

*C. D10 and D30*

*D. D10 and D30*

**Q.300 Coastal zone occupies________**

*A. 15%*

*B. 25%*

*C. Less than 15%*

*D. Less than 25%*

**Q.301 Which of the following reservoirs contains the most water?**

*A. Atmosphere*

*B. Biosphere*

*C. Groundwater*

*D. Lakes and rivers*

**Q.302 Pick the non-planar fold from the following.**

*A. Box fold*

*B. Cheveron fold*

*C. Conjugate fold*

*D. Cuspate fold*

**Q.303 Pick the option which is not the cause of folding.**

*A. Folding due to tangential tension*

*B. Folding due to tangential compression*

*C. Folding due to intrusions*

*D. Folding due to differential compression*

**Q.304 For an ideal Rigid building, Time Period is**

*A. greater than zero*

*B. greater than 1*

*C. less than zero*

*D. Equal to zero*

**Q.305 How does the thickness of the layer affect flexural folding?**

*A. thinner the layers, greater is the slip*

*B. thicker the layers, lesser is the slip*

*C. thicker the layers, greater is the slip*

*D. has no effect*

**Q.306 Which of the following need not be avoided for construction of quake resistant buildings?**

A. *Uniform height*

B. *Chimneys*

C. *Heavy weight walls*

D. *Discontinuous foundations*

**Q.307 What is the difference between dolomite and calcite?**

A. *Dolomite is calcium carbonate and calcite are magnesium carbonate*

B. *Dolomite is calcium - magnesium carbonate and calcite are calcium carbonate*

C. *Dolomite is calcium- magnesium carbonate and calcite are magnesium carbonate*

D. *Dolomite is magnesium carbonate and calcite are calcium carbonate*

**Q.308 What will result in an offset with a gap?**

A. *Downthrow to left side*

B. *Upthrow to left side*

C. *Downthrow to right side*

D. *Upthrow to right side*

**Q.309 The wavelength of tsunami in deep water is:**

A. *Large*

B. *Short*

C. *none of these*

**Q.310 Speed of shallow water wave depends upon water depth as:**

A. *directly to its square*

B. *directly to its under root*

C. *inversely to its square*

D. *inversely to its under root*

**Q.311 Why tsunami is not easily noticeable in deep ocean:**

A. *because of its wavelength*

B. *because of its source*

C. *None of these*

**Q.312 A wave is called shallow water wave when the wavelength is:**

A. *very large as compared to water depth*

B. *small as compared to water depth*

C. *equal to that of water depth*

**Q.313 The wavelength of tsunami wave depends upon:**

A. *generating mechanism*

B. *dimensions of the source event*

C. *both of the above*

**Q.314 If the tsunami is generated from a large earthquake over a large area, then its wavelength will be:**

A. *Greater*

B. *Shorter*

C. *None of these*

**Q.315 The wavelength of tsunami wave depends upon water depth as**

A. *directly proportional to its square*

B. *directly proportional to its cube*

C. *inversely proportional to its one-fourth power*

D. *inversely proportional to its cube*

**Q.316 By what factor will the wavelength of tsunami wave will change in shallow water if depth of shallow water changed from 2m to 32m:**

A. *2*

*B. 4*

*C. 8D. 16*

**Q.317 The point where the energy is released during the earthquake is called?**

*A. Epicenter*

*B. Hypo center*

*C. Circumcenter*

*D. None of the above*

**Q.318 The sensitivity of gravimeters can be increased by**

*A. Increasing the mass and increasing the spring constant*

*B. Increasing the mass and decreasing the spring constant*

*C. Decreasing the mass and increasing the spring constant*

*D. Decreasing the mass and decreasing the spring constant*

**Q.319 As seismic wavelet propagates further and further through a rock medium, what happens to its amplitude spectrum?**

*A. Increases overall*

*B. Decreases overall, and gets narrower due to greater loss of higher frequencies.*

*C. Remains constant*

*D. None of the above*

**Q.320 Which zone is at top of all the other zones?**

*A. soil water zone*

*B. saturated zone*

*C. intermediate zone*

*D. capillary zone*

**Q.321 What occurs due to falling of big rock blocks or sides due to release of stresses during tunnelling?**

*A. Rock fall*

*B. Rock bursts*

*C. Blockage*

*D. Water rush*

**Q.322 What is the range of grain size for coarse grained igneous rock?**

*A. Above 2 mm*

*B. Below 2 mm*

*C. Above 5 mm*

*D. Below 5 mm*

**Q.323 Which process involves either a physical or chemical breakdown of earth materials?**

*A. deposition*

*B. sedimentation*

*C. weathering*

*D. cementing*

**Q.324 What is the average depth of ocean?**

*A. Approx 4 km*

*B. Less than 4 km*

*C. Greater than 4 km*

*D. None of these*

**Q.325 In which cause of folding, the thickness of fold does not remain uniform?**

*A. flexural folding*

*B. shear folding*

*C. flowage folding*

*D. flexural folding*

**Q.326 Where is geothermal method used?**

*A. For the measurement of temperature on the surface of earth, in shallow holes or in deep bore holes.*
*B. In deep structural analysis, ore deposits, groundwater studies,*
*C. For delineation of salt water- fresh water interfaces etc.*
*D. All of the above*

**Q.327 What is the name for the type of unconformity that James Hutton described at sicar point, Scotland?**

*A. Disconformity*
*B. Nonconformity*
*C. Angular unconformity*
*D. Paraconformity*

**Q.328 Which of the following is not true about a mineral?**

*A. Naturally occurring*
*B. Inorganic substance*
*C. Organic substance*
*D. Definite chemical composition*

## ***Answers***

| 1 | 2 | 3 | 4 | 5 | 6 | 7 | 8 | 9 | 10 |
|---|---|---|---|---|---|---|---|---|---|
| D | A | C | A | C | C | A | D | C | A |
| 11 | 12 | 13 | 14 | 15 | 16 | 17 | 18 | 19 | 20 |
| A | B | B | C | B | C | C | C | D | C |
| 21 | 22 | 23 | 24 | 25 | 26 | 27 | 28 | 29 | 30 |
| A | B | A | B | D | D | B | A | B | B |
| 31 | 32 | 33 | 34 | 35 | 36 | 37 | 38 | 39 | 40 |
| B | A | A | B | C | D | B | D | C | C |
| 41 | 42 | 43 | 44 | 45 | 46 | 47 | 48 | 49 | 50 |
| C | A | A | C | A, B | D | A | C | B | A |
| 51 | 52 | 53 | 54 | 55 | 56 | 57 | 58 | 59 | 60 |
| C | D | B | D | A | D | C | A | B | A |
| 61 | 62 | 63 | 64 | 65 | 66 | 67 | 68 | 69 | 70 |
| D | A | B | C | B | A | C | C | D | A |
| 71 | 72 | 73 | 74 | 75 | 76 | 77 | 78 | 79 | 80 |
| A | B | C | C | B | B | C | A | A | C |
| 81 | 82 | 83 | 84 | 85 | 86 | 87 | 88 | 89 | 90 |
| A,B,C | B,C | A | B | C | D | D | A | A | A |
| 91 | 92 | 93 | 94 | 95 | 96 | 97 | 98 | 99 | 100 |
| A,C,D | C | A | A | A,D | A | A | A | A | ALL |
| 101 | 102 | 103 | 104 | 105 | 106 | 107 | 108 | 109 | 110 |
| C | C | B | A,C,D | B | A | A,B,D | C | A | D |
| 111 | 112 | 113 | 114 | 115 | 116 | 117 | 118 | 119 | 120 |
| C | C | A | B | C | A | A | D | C | B |
| 121 | 122 | 123 | 124 | 125 | 126 | 127 | 128 | 129 | 130 |
| B | A | B | C | D | B | A | D | C | A |
| 131 | 132 | 133 | 134 | 135 | 136 | 137 | 138 | 139 | 140 |
| A | C | B | C | C | A | B | B | C | B |
| 141 | 142 | 143 | 144 | 145 | 146 | 147 | 148 | 149 | 150 |
| A | B | C | C | D | C | D | A | A | B |
| 151 | 152 | 153 | 154 | 155 | 156 | 157 | 158 | 159 | 160 |
| C | A | A | A | B | B | C | A | A | C |
| 161 | 162 | 163 | 164 | 165 | 166 | 167 | 168 | 169 | 170 |
| C | A | C | A | C | C | A | C | A | A |
| 171 | 172 | 173 | 174 | 175 | 176 | 177 | 178 | 179 | 180 |
| D | A | C | A | D | D | B | C | D | D |
| 181 | 182 | 183 | 184 | 185 | 186 | 187 | 188 | 189 | 190 |
| D | D | C | D | A | B | A | A | A | B |
| 191 | 192 | 193 | 194 | 195 | 196 | 197 | 198 | 199 | 200 |
| C | C | B | A | C | C | B | D | B | C |
| 201 | 202 | 203 | 204 | 205 | 206 | 207 | 208 | 209 | 210 |
| A | C | A | A | C | B | B | A | D | A |
| 211 | 212 | 213 | 214 | 215 | 216 | 217 | 218 | 219 | 220 |
| A | A,C | C | A | A | C | D | D | C | B |
| 221 | 222 | 223 | 224 | 225 | 226 | 227 | 228 | 229 | 230 |
| B | B | B | C | A | A | C | C | A | B |
| 231 | 232 | 233 | 234 | 235 | 236 | 237 | 238 | 239 | 240 |
| B | A | B | D | D | A | C | A | D | B |
| 241 | 242 | 243 | 244 | 245 | 246 | 247 | 248 | 249 | 250 |
| C | A | B | C | A | A | B | D | B | C |
| 251 | 252 | 253 | 254 | 255 | 256 | 257 | 258 | 259 | 260 |
| B | C | A | D | C | B | C | D | B | B |
| 261 | 262 | 263 | 264 | 265 | 266 | 267 | 268 | 269 | 270 |
| C | B | D | A | C | B | A | A,B | C,D | B |
| 271 | 272 | 273 | 274 | 275 | 276 | 277 | 278 | 279 | 280 |
| D | D | A | D | C | A | B | A | D | A |
| 281 | 282 | 283 | 284 | 285 | 286 | 287 | 288 | 289 | 290 |
| C | A | D | C | C | C | B | C | A | D |
| 291 | 292 | 293 | 294 | 295 | 296 | 297 | 298 | 299 | 300 |
| B | A | B | D | C | D | A | B | A | C |
| 301 | 302 | 303 | 304 | 305 | 306 | 307 | 308 | 309 | 310 |
| C | A | A | D | C | A | B | C | B | B |
| 311 | 312 | 313 | 314 | 315 | 316 | 317 | 318 | 319 | 320 |
| C | A | C | A | C | A | B | C | B | A |
| 321 | 322 | 323 | 324 | 325 | 326 | 327 | 328 | 329 | |
| B | C | C | C | C | D | C | C | B | |

# TWO

# SEGMENT-2 SHORT Q & A

1. What are some examples of neutral refractories?
Ans: Zirconia
2. Should a refractory material posses thermal expansion property?
Ans: Yes.
3. What percentage of the iron and steel industry are using refractories.?
Ans: 70%.
4.Fixed bed reactor is an example of?
Ans: Continuous reactor
5. Matte smelting is generally used for which type of ore?
Ans: Sulphidic ore
6. Which element is the most commonly used reducing agent?
Ans: Carbon
7. The impeller according to their speed :
Ans: turbine>propeller>paddle
8. What does the velocity of particle in a fluid medium depends on?
SIZE,SPECIFIC GRAVITY, SHAPE OF THE PARTICLE
9. What are some examples of Basic Refractories?
CaO, MgO.
10. What are some properties of Refractories?
Strength, porosity, chemical inertness.
11. What are some uses of Refractories?
Used in furnaces, kilns, reactors.
12. What is Porosity?
Ans: Porosity is the ratio of its pore's volume to the bulk volume.
13. Should a refractory be resistive to corrosion?
Yes. Good refractory must show a good resistance to abrasion or corrosion.
14. What is abrasion?
A damaged area of a skin where it has been rubbed against something hard or rough.
15. All Metallurgical processes are?
Ans: Heterogeneous in nature.
16. How many types of reactors on the basis of rate of feeding and rate of product formation?
Ans: 2, Continuous and discontinuous
17. Which type of reactor is preferred?
Continuous because it increases the productivity
18. What is the most favourable advantage of electric arc furnaces?
Ans: There are no combustion gases

19. Why the word fix is added in fix bed reactors?
Ans: Bcoz it contains a fixed bed of catalyst
20. When a reverberatory furnace used?
Ans: When direct contact between reaction gases and raw materials is to be avoided.
21. Which material is used in electric arc furnaces as electrodes?
Ans: Carbon or graphite
22. What is retention time?
Ans: Time duration for which the material has stayed within the reactor
23. What is a relation to average retention time?
M/m where M is a mass inside the reactor and m is the feeding rate.
24. Name the types of furnaces in which matte smelting can be carried out.
Ans: Reverberatory furnace and flash smelter
25. Among reverberatory furnace and flash smelter which o e is better to be used and why?
Ans: Flash smelter because of high recovery of metals with low investment and operating costs.
26. Why there is no reducing agent used in matte smelting?
Ans: Because sulphide present in matte itself acts as reducing agent
27. Reduction smelting is carried out in _______ and ________ furnace
Ans: Blast and electric furnace
28. Among blast furnace and electric arc furnace which one is eco - friendly?
Ans: Electric arc furnace
29. During smelting of iron limestone serve the purpose of __________
Ans: Flux
30. Complete the reaction
$CaO+SiO_2$ ---->??
Ans: $CaSiO_3$(slag formed during smelting of iron)
31. ______ serve the purpose of burning fuel during smelting of iron.
Ans: Coke ($2C + O_2$ ------>$2CO$)
32. How many factors depends on velocity of particle in fluid medium?
Ans: Velocity of particle in fluid medium depends on three factors.
33. What is viscous resistance?
Ans: Resistance is due to shear force and viscosity.
34. what is turbulent resistance?
Ans: Resistance is due to displacement.
35. what is value of acceleration at the terminal velocity?
Ans: Zero.
36. How much drag force acting on a spherical particle due to viscous resistance?
Ans: $D=3\Pi dnv$.
Where n=fluid viscosity, v=terminal velocity.
37. Where Newton's law is applicable in mixture of minerals?
Ans: Newton's law is valid for particles larger than about 0.5Cm in diameter.
38. Where Stoke's law is valid in mixture of minerals?
Ans: Stoke's law is valid for particles below about 50 micro meter in diameter.
39. On which principle wet classifiers works?
Ans: Separation of coarse particles from fine by liquid fluidization.
40. On which principle dry classifiers works?
Ans: Separation by air fluidzation
41. Which is a primary stage in the extraction of a metal from an ore?
Ans: Ore dressing

42. The primary processes of comminution are____?
Ans: crushing & grinding
43. Compression and impact forces are extensively used in?
Ans: crushing operation
44. The dominant force in grinding is?
Ans: attrition
45. The working principle of jaw crusher is based on?
Ans: pressure crushing
46. The function of eccentric rotating drive shaft is to produce ________ in movable jaw.
Ans: oscillation
47. Gyratory crushers are suitable for crushing?
Ans: large boulders
48. Which parameter is altered to get the reduced size of product particle in ball mill is?
Ans: speed
49. Power consumption in ball mill depends upon the material inside ball mill and ______?
Ans: the bond work index of the material
50. Dry grinding is preferred method for grinding of?
Ans: light and soft materials
51. Wet grinding is preferred method for grinding of?
Ans: hard and heavy materials
52. What is used for fuel in bath smelting?
Ans: Non -caking Coal
53. Which type of feed used in bath smelting?
Ans: Fine ore
54. What is the product of DIOS bath smelting?
Ans: Hot metal(Liquid iron).
55. Which process has lower energy consumption?
Ans: Bath smelting process compare to blast furnace and others.
56. What is product of corex process?
Ans: Liquid sponge iron
57. Name two types of air pulsated jig used in coal industry?
Ans: Baum and Bata jig.
58. Liquid- liquid mixture is seperated by solvent extraction using____________ solvent.
Ans: Immiscible
59. Solvent extraction is more effective when the extraction is repeated with?
Ans: Small solvent
60. A system which requires less solvent and produces more concentrated exractant phase has:
Ans: Large distribution coefficient
61. The effectiveness of a solvent can be measured by:
Ans: Diffusion coefficient and selectivity
62. Which type of LLE is more effective?
Ans: Multistage counter current
63. For solvent extraction the selectivity is desired to be
Ans: Larger than 1
64. Two phase aqueous extraction requires:
Ans: Low surface tension
65. The minimum density difference Between heavier and lighter phase required
Ans: 5 percent

66. In Matte Smelting and Converting Iron and sulphur are
Ans: Oxidised
67. What happens to activity of FeS with increasing oxygen potential
Ans: Decreases
68. What is formula of white metal
Ans: $Cu_2S$
69. What is the product of further oxidation of White metal
Ans: Blister copper
70. What is the percentage of sulphur in blister copper
Ans: About 1%
71. Activity of FeS for co existance of blister copper and white metal
Ans: 0.1
72. Which gas is produced in matte smelting
Ans: $SO_2$
73. What is added to matte to avoid production of $SO_2$?
Ans: CaO or limestone
74. What causes blister in copper
Ans: Evolving of $SO_2$
75. What is the intermediate product of matte smelting
Ans: Magnetite
76. Types of primary crushers?
Ans: Jaw and Gyratory crushers
77. Types of secondary crushers ?
Ans: Cone, roll and impact crushers
78. Types of tumbling mills ?
Ans: Rod, ball and auto-genous mills
79. Most widely used secondary crusher ?
Ans: Cone crusher
80. Types of jaw crushers ?
Ans: Dodge, blake and universal
81. Types of blake crushers ?
Ans: Single toggle and double toggle blake crusher
82. Types of impact crushers ?
Ans: Hammer mill, impact mill and vertical shaft impactors
83. Tensile fracturing of materials ouucurs at:-
Ans: Low level of stress
84. Causes of progressively form of the failure plane are:-
Ans: Micro cracks and natural heterogeneities
85. A rock material contains a large number of randomly orientated zones of potential failure in the form of
Ans: Grain boundaries
86. Brittle fracture occurs in materials with high strength and
Ans: Low ductility
87. Plastic deformation occurs before fracturing in
Ans: Ductile fracture
88. Most of hard rocks like limestone exhibit
Ans: Brittle behaviour
89. The easiest way of generating high stresses is by
Ans: Dynamic impact forces

90. Tensile failure of rocks generates

Ans: Coarse fragments

91. Crack propagation is originated from areas of induced

Ans: Tension

92. Compressive-shear breakage produces

Ans: Finer fragments

93. Why does the particle crowding is negligible in free settling?

Ans: Sinking of particles in Volume of fluid is large with respect to total volume of particles

94. What did newton law say about drag force?

Ans: Due to turbulent resistance

95. What is particle size to obey stokes law?

Ans: 50 micrometer

96. The terminal velocity of a particle in a particular fluid in stokes and newton law is function defined only on which attributes?

Ans: Particle size and density

97. Which particle will have larger terminal velocity if they same density?

Ans: Larger diameter

98. The expression of free settling ratio is given by?

Ans: da/db = [(Db-Df)/Da-Df)]^n

99. When does the greater reduction in falling velocity is seen?

Ans: Greater reduction in Ds-Dp

100. Which settling ratio is bigger?

Ans: Hinder settling ratio

101. What does hinder setting reduces and what it's effect?

Ans: Reduces effect of size and this inturn increases effect of density on classification

102. What is the principle of zone refining?

Ans: Zone refining is based on the principle of Fractional Crystallization.

103. What is Liquation?

Ans: It is a process of selective melting of a component in an ore or alloy.

104. Give examples of Distillation?

Ans: Separate Hydrocarbons from crude oil, Kerosene, Gasoline

105. Give examples of Liquation?

Ans: Lead, Tin, Mercury are refined using Liquation.

106. Give examples of Zone refining?

Ans: Silicon and Gallium are refined using Zone refining.

107. Give examples of Fire refining?

Ans: Iron,Lead,Tin,Copper are refined using Fire refining.

108. What is the thermodynamics & kinetic advantage of hydrogen plasma?

Ans: Hydrogen plasma is reduction favourable at low temperature and it has low activation energy.

109. By which in hydrogen plasma thermodynamic & kinetic advantage occur?

Ans: By vibrationally excited molecular ($H_2^*$), atomic H & ionic ($H^+$) .

110. Why SRM &waste polyethylene terephthlate uses as reducing agent?

Ans: Because it has presence of Carbon & Hydrogen atom.

111. On which property of matter is jigging process based?

Ans: Density

112. At what pulse rate, Jigging process will have mximum efficiency keeping other factors unchanged?

Ans: Natural frequency of lighter particles

113. In Jigging of coal, the coal particles are removed as tailings or settled at the bottoom as concentrates?

Ans: Removed as tailings

114. Name two air pulsated jigs used in coal industry.

Ans: Baum and Batac

115. What special condition is required for working of InLine pressure jigs?

Ans: Elevated temperature

116. What special force is aided for speration process in Kelsey Jigs?

Ans: Centrifugal force

117. What is the significant change in IHC jig drive compared to conventional jig drive?

Ans: It has asymmetrical saw tooth movement

118. Which happens if the the hutch water level is beyond the optimum level?

Ans: Washes fine heavies to tailings

119. Name a ragging material used for gold jigs.

Ans: Lead shots

120. What is the downward movement of water called in a jig cycle?

Ans: Suction

121. Give a example of Heterogeneous catalysis .

Ans: Haber-Bosch process.

122. In Haber-Bosch process, which gas has been used?

Ans: ammonia

123. Example of Metallothermic reduction reaction.

Ans: Reduction of Fe2O3 by Aluminum (Thermite Welding).

124. What is kroll's process?

Ans: Reduction of Halides of Titanium (TiCl4) by Magnesium (Mg) to produce metallic Ti.

125. Which reducing gas is used in reduction of iron ore?

Ans: Mixture of gas consisting $H_2$ and CO (Syngas).

126. What are the two-intermediate oxide in reduction of Hematite ore to Iron?

Ans: Magnetite(Fe3O4) and Wustite(Fe0.95O).

127. What is the geometry of shaft furnace?

Ans: Cylindrical in reduction and transition section while conical in cooling section.

128. What is Direct Reduced Iron?

Ans: It is the Iron formed after reduction process of iron ore and also called sponge iron.

129. Mineral processing is also known as?

Ans: Ore dressing

130. Classification is done on the basis of?

Ans: Settling velocity of particles in water or air.

131. Velocity of a particle in fluid medium depends on?

Ans: Size, specific gravity and shape of particle

132. Name types of classifiers.

Ans: Wet and dry classifier

133. Principle on which wet classifier works?

Ans: Separation of coarse particle from fine particle by liquid fluidisztion

134. Coarse partice moves faster than fine particle. True/false

Ans: TRUE

135. High density particle move faster than low density particle of equal size. True/False

Ans: TRUE

136. Difference between hydrolic classifier and sedimentation classifier.

Ans: In hydrolic classifier particle settling direction is in opposite direction.

137. Which process is economically feasible?

Ans: Bath smelting compare to blast furnace and other process.

138. Is there any need of sintering plant for feed in bath smelting?

Ans: No because we use fine ore in bath smelting

139. Which process harm the atmosphere very less?

Ans: Bath smelting

140. What are different type of coal?

Ans: 4 types
Non- caking, caking, Non- coking, Coking

141. Which hydroxy oxime is most suitable for copper extraction from zinc solution ?

Ans: LIX-984

142. Why is fluidized bed used in cadmium extraction in the SX technique?

Ans: To minimise the use of zinc dust.

143. Name a toxic product formed during the cementation process of zinc solution.

Ans: AsH3(Arsine)

144. How zinc gets electrowon from zinc sulfate solution despite having more negative reduction potential than hydrogen?

Ans: Because hydrogen evolution has a large over potential on zinc metal .

145. Which compound is added to accelerate the extraction of cobalt from the galvanic cell of zinc dust and copper particles?

Ans: Arsenious oxide

146. Write down the principle of following method:- (a) Zone Refining

Ans: In zone refining impurities are more soluble in molten state than in solid state.

147. How many metals are commercially purified by van arkel method from the given metals ...

Na, Ag, Ti, Bi, Zr, Pb, Hg
Ans: Ti, Bi, Zr

148. Which process is matte smelting?

Ans: Oxidation

149. Intermediate product of matte smelting and converting

Ans: Solid Magnetite

150. What is the slag forming oxides?

Ans: FeO and SO2

151. What is the activity of FeS at low oxygen potential?

Ans: 1-0.1

152. Which has causes blister in copper?

Ans: SO2

153. What is the percentage of sulphur in blister copper for coexistence with White metal?

Ans: 1

154. Activity of FeS for co existance between White metal and blister copper?

Ans: 0.1

155. When copper is roast with lime what is the product

Ans: CuS

156. Where Matte is converted to metallic copper

Ans: Pierce Smith Converter

157. What is residence time?

Ans: The amount of time a molecule spends in a reactor.

158. What is micro mixing?

Ans: micro mixing is a process in which ingredient particles rearrange to form a blend.

159. Write an application for the Ellingham Diagram.

Ans: it helps in predicting the feasibility of thermal reduction of an ore

160. In manufacturing of iron , lime stone added to the furnace, the calcium ion ends in the form of?

Ans: Slag

161. In manufacturing of iron from Hematite, the function of lime stone is as?

Ans: Flux

162. What happens when zinc carbonate is calcined?

Ans: Carbonate ore on calcination gives out C02 and forms oxide which can be reduced using carbon

163. Moisture content is dependent on?

Ans: moisture content decreases with time

164. What is the condition for constant drying?

Ans: Constant temperature, Constant Humidity & Constant velocity.

165. Find the gas phase mass transfer co-efficient for a unbound moisture to remove if the flux is 5 kg/sq.m sec and then difference in humidity of the liquid and the main stream is 0.5 units.

Ans: Flux =Ys-Y
mass transfer co-efficient =5/0.5=10

166. Calculate the flux (kg/sq.m sec) if mass of dry solid =8kg wet surface area =4 sq.m; charge with moisture content with time is 0.4/sec.

Ans: Flux= 8/4 *0.4 =0.8

167. What type of separators are used to treat ferromagnetic materials and some highly paramagnetic materials?

Ans: Low intensity magnetic separators

168. What is force factor?

Ans: Product of applied magnetic field strength and magnetic field gradient

169. Depending upon the magnetic field gradient what are the types of magnetic separators?

Ans: Open gradient magnetic separator (OGMS) and High gradient magnetic separator (HGMS)

170. What are the main benefits of magnetic separators?

Ans: Simple and efficient, incredibly versatile and high production rate

171. What are the methods of electrostatic charging of particles?

Ans: Ion Bombardment, Conductive induction and contact charging

172. What is the motion of charged particles under the influence of electric field is called?

Ans: Electrophoresis

173. What are the factors affecting the electrostatic separation process?

Ans: Intensity of electric field, particle size, relative humidity, temperature of particle, inter electrode distance

174. What are the different types of electrostatic separator?

Ans: High tension roll separator, plate or screen separator

175. What is the function of wilfley shaking table?

Ans: for the recovery of precious metals from low tonnage streams etc

176. State any advantages of shaking table?

Ans: Highly selective, with high upgrading ratio if used correctly.

177. How does grade value ditermined?

Ans: By the liberation of surface area of the valuable minerals.

178. How settling rate and particle size is related?

Ans: finer the particles slower is the settling rate.

179. Principle behind washing process?

Ans: density difference

180. Principle behind precipitation process?

Ans: converting soluble compound to insoluble one.

181. Basic difference between electrowinning and electrorefining?

Ans: in electrowinning anode is inert whereas in electrorefining anode is impure metal.

182. Give some examples of metals which can be produced by metallothermic reduction reaction.

Ans: Magnesium, titanium, zirconium, beryllium, tantalum, neodyium. etc

183. What is included in the charge to produce coarse particles?

Ans: Calcium chloride

184. In what mole ratio, the calcined material and reductant are mixed and pelletized?

Ans: CaO: Al = 3: 2

185. What is ferroniobium?

Ans: It is an iron-niobium alloy.

186. What do you mean by pelletization?

Ans: It is a process of compressing or molding a material into the shape of a pellet.

187. Which leaching reagent is used in the extraction of gold?

Ans: NaCN solution is used.

188. Vat leaching is suitable for which types of materials?

Ans: It is suitable for porous and sandy materials.

189. What is the reducing agent used in smelting process?

Ans: Coke or charcoal

190. Why molten mattes are insoluble in both slag and metal phases?

Ans: Because of difference in specific gravities.

191. How slag is disposed off in matte smelting ?

Ans: Slag is lighter so it floats on the surface.

192. What are properties of slag used in matte smelting?

Ans: Immiscible with matte phase, good fluidity and low solubility of Cu2S in matte phase.

193. How to achieve the qualities mentioned in previous question in slag?

Ans: By keeping viscosity as low as possible.

194. What is the use of a converter?

Ans: Selection oxidation of matte and leave copper as metal.

195. Which converter is used in extraction of copper?

Ans: Pierce-Smith converter

196. Which flux is added for iron removal during converting?

Ans: Silica

197. What is the drawback of matte smelting process?

Ans: SO2 is produced in large quantities which needs to be disposed off.

198. How to avoid the problem in previous question?

Ans: By roasting copper concentrate in presence of lime or limestone.

199. What is the shape of hydrolic classifier?

Ans: Conical and Cylindrical

200. What is the overflow capacity of hydrolic classifier?

Ans: 50%

201. Name two types of sedimentation classifier.

Ans: Spiral and Rake classifier

202. Where are the raw materials fed in sedimentation classifier?

Ans: Central section of the pool

203. What is implemented to clean coarse material?

Ans: Water

204. How does partical fall downwards in hydrocylone?

Ans: Tangentially

205. Dry classifier is based on which type of principle?

Ans: Air fluidisation

206. How does purification is done in air classification?

Ans: By aerodynamic property

207. What types of force come into action in dry classifier?

Ans: Drag force and Gravitational force

208. Which particle is suspended in air streams in dry classifier?

Ans: Higher drag to weight ratio

209. What is stoke's law?

Ans: The expression v=gd^2(Ds-Df)/18n is known as stokes law.

210. What are granulated materials?

Ans: These are composed of grains in contact and are discontinuous and heterogeneous.

211. Which process is favorable?

Ans: Use continuous processing instead of batch processing.

212. How can electricity be used as a fuel?

Ans: Electricity can be used as a great source to melt and alloy metals and refractories.

213. Alternative reductants which is uses at industrial level?

Ans: SRM,Charcoal from agriculture residue, waste polyethylene terephthlate, Hydrogen

214. Alternative reductants which is not uses at industrial level?

Ans: Hydrogen plasma

215. Why some problem occur in iron making by SRM?

Ans: Presence of Cu in SRM.

216. How is thermodynamic feasibility of cementation determined?

Ans: By the ratio of the electrode potentials.

217. Why does copper precipitates before iron in the zinc cementation process?

Ans: Cu gets extracted at pH values greater than 5 where as iron requires a pH level greater than 8.

218. Why are porcelain pieces used in distillation?

Ans: They provide a large uneven surface for vapour bubble to form during the boiling process.

219. What is the principal of fractional distillation?

Ans: It works on the principal that different liquids boil at different temperatures.

220. Give one example of fractional distillation

Ans: Separation of crude oil into various products such as gasoline.

221. Which method is best to separate ethanol water mixture?

Ans: Fractional distillation because the boiling point of ethanol is much lower than that of water.

222. What is the use of a still?

Ans: It contains reboilers or pots in which the source material is heated.

223. A mineral breaks along preferred directions called

Ans: Cleavage

224. __________ is not a form of intrusive igneous

Ans: Concordant

225. Pick the plutonic igneous rock

Ans: Granite

226. The rocks which exhibit mixed characteristics of volcanic and plutonic rocks are

Ans: Hypabyssal rocks

227. Plutonic rocks are formed at depths below the Earth's surface ranging

Ans: 7 to 10 kilometres

228. The main constituent in igneous rocks is

Ans: Silica

229. The layered arrangement in sedimentary rocks is called __________

Ans: Stratification

230. The structure most prevalent to clastic rocks is ___________

Ans: Lamination

231. Lamination is structure formed in which type of sedimentary rocks?

Ans: Fine grained

232. Each layer of a laminated structure of sedimentary rock is called ?

Ans: Lamina

233. Which among the following is not a type of false bedding?

Ans: Columnar

234. The type of false bedding where top and bottom surfaces are parallel is ___________

Ans: Tabular

235. Type of false bedding where the individual layers exist in well-defined sets of parallel layers is ___________

Ans: Wedge shaped

236. Type of bedding where sorting and arrangement has occurred based on grain size is?

Ans: Graded bedding

237. Graded bedding occurs due to which phenomenon?

Ans: Gravitational settling

238. The texture of a soil is determined by the soil particles'

Ans: Chemical makeup

239. Rusting is caused by ...

Ans: Oxidation

# THREE

# SEGMENT-3 Q & A

### *How fine do screens get?*

*This depends on the thickness of the wire or strand used to make the mesh. Most Industrial Specialities Mfg. flow control components do not contain filter screens any finer than 500 mesh. The primary reason for this is that as the mesh number rises, the space between the wires or strands becomes smaller. At some point, the mesh number becomes so high that the percentage of open area is too low to be useful. This point is usually somewhere between 450 and 700 mesh depending on the diameter of the wire or filament used.*

### *What is the moisture content in the feed material to be screened?*

*No matter if the moisture content is 5%, 10%, 20% or bone dry (0% moisture), it is a significant factor that can determine the type and size of the screening unit. It also allows the manufacturer to provide recommendations critical to achieving maximum screening efficiency.*

### *What is the mechanism of mixing and describe it?*

*Three basic mechanisms:-*

- ***Convection**:- movement of a group of particles because of the direct action of an impeller or moving device. Example- trough mixer with spiral ribbon*
- ***Diffusion**:- diffusion refers to the random dispersion of individual particles in the inter-particle void spaces throughout the mixer. Example- simple barrel mixture*
- ***Shear mixing**:- groups of particles are mixed through the formation of slipping planes developed by the action of the blade. newly formed slipping planes in turn allow particles to diffuse through new void spaces.*

### *What is the rate of mixing and write the equation of mixing?*

*The rate of mixing at any time under constant working conditions ought to be proportional to the extent of mixing remaining to be done at that time equation is*

$$dM/dt=K(1-M) \text{ where M is the rate of mixing}$$

### *Write the name of a type of agitator or impeller?*

*Type of agitator /impeller –*

- *Paddle,*
- *Propeller,*
- *Turbine.*

## *Two types of movement of particle in fluid?*

- *Free and*
- *Hindered movement*

## *Name types of wet classifier*

- Hydrocyclone,hydraulic classifier and Sedimentation classifier

## *Write the short notes about propeller ?*

1. Primarily used to blend low viscosity liquids.
2. Impeller diameter is much smaller than that of turbine mixers.
3. The mixer shaft is usually positioned on an angle and off centre.
4. Two are more propellers are used for deep tank.

## *Mineral processing can involve four general types of unit operations. What are they?*

1. Comminution- the process of particles size reduction.
2. Sizing - separation of particle size by screening
3. Dewatering - solid liquid separation.
4. Concentration by taking advantage of physical and surface chemical properties.

## *Write the short notes about turbine?*

1. They resembles multi bladed paddle agitators with short blades, turning at high speeds on a shaft mounted centrally in the vessel.
2. Blades may be straight or curved, pitched or vertical.
3. Diameter of impeller turbine is smaller than with paddles, ranging from 30 to 50% of vessel diameter.

## *What is viscous resistance?*

- Resistance when the velocity of decent is LOW, causing the resistance to be only due to shear force and viscosity. This type of resistance is called viscous resistance

### *What is turbulent resistance?*

- Resistance when the velocity of decent is HIGH, resistance being caused only due to displacement of the particle. This type of resistance is known as turbulent resistance.

### *What are the forces acting on a particle submerged in a liquid?*

- Gravitational force
- Upward buoyant force due to the displaced fluid
- Drag force D acting upward

### *What are the different types of classifiers, how can they be differentiated based on the direction of flow of carrying current?*

Two types (depending on the direction of flow of carrying current)

1. Horizontal current classifier or mechanical classifier are essentially of free settling type and accenture the sizing function
2. Vertical current or Hydraulic classifier are usually hindered settling types and so increase the effect of density on separation

### *Why is the size of each successive column increased in a hydraulic classifier?*

- The size is increased as the amt of liquid to be handled by the next vessel is increased. Another reason is the requirement to reduce the surface velocity of fluid flowing from one vessel to another.

### *What will be the effect of increasing feed rate in a horizontal current classifier.*

- Increasing feed rate increases horizontal carrying velocity thus increases size of particle in overflow

### *How does the speed of rakes determine the degree of agitation of pulp?*

- Increasing the speed of rakes increases the degree of agitation causing the overflow to contain more fines and vice versa.

## *What is the advantage of hindered setteling classifier over free setteling classifier?*

- Hindered setteling classifier uses much less water than the free settling type and is more selective in action.
- Free settling is rarely used as it is inefficient in sizing and sorting.

## *What is terminal velocity?*

- Terminal velocity is the velocity at which the drag force of the particle equals that of the acceleration due to gravity.

## *How could the production of large quantity of SO2 be avoided in matte smelting?*

- In order to avoid the production, we need to roast copper concentrate in the presence of lime or limestone which captures sulphur as CaS or CaSO4. Thus, metallic copper is produced while capturing all sulphur.

## *What is Blister copper?*

- At the end of matte smelting and converting process, the copper sulphide has been completely oxidised to metallic copper and sulphur dioxide. The resulting product is Blister copper which has 98.5% pure copper and is named so as when solidified copper contains blisters due to evolution of SO2.

## *How silica plays important role in immiscibility of matte and slag?*

- When silica is absent oxide and sulphide form one covalently bonded phase (Cu-Fe-O-S). When Si is present it combines with oxides to formed silicate polymer anion which together to form slag. While sulphides show no tendency to form complex anion. Thus, separating matte and slag.

## *Why is viscosity of slag kept as low as possible?*

- Because slag would entrap more droplet of matte if viscosity is higher thus separation becomes difficult of matte and slag.

## *What are the properties of slag?*

1. Immiscible with matte
2. Low solubility of $Cu_2S$ in slag
3. Good fluidity

## *What is matte and slag composed of?*

- The silica , alumina,iron oxide, calcium oxide and other minor oxide form slag. While copper, sulphur , unoxidised iron , precious metals form matte.

## *What is matte?*

- It is term given to molten metal sulphide phase in which principal metal being extracted to recovered prior to final reduction process to produce crude metal.

## *What is roast reduction?*

- It is process in which sulphide ore is roasted and the resultant oxide is reduced with carbon to form metallic copper in case of iron- copper mattes.

## *Effect of temperature- oxygen potential in isolating copper in matte?*

- A high smelting temperature (>1200 C) leads to fluid slag, a clear-cut matte- slag separation and low copper losses in slag. High oxidising conditions lead to high copper losses in slag.

## *Reducing agent used in smelting process? And How?*

- Carbon in form of coke and charcoal act the reducing agent. Carbon oxides in two stages carbon monoxide and carbon dioxide , thus removing oxygen from the ore leaving the elemental metal.

## *What is classification?*

- Classification is separation of mixtures of minerals into two or more products on the basis of the velocity with which grains fall through a fluid medium.

## *How many types of classifiers?*

Two types of classifiers

1. Mechanical classifier
2. Hydraulic classifier

## *Define classification.*

- It is method of separating mixture of mineral particles into two or more products according to their settling velocity in water or air.

## *Where is gravity method of Investigation useful?*

Gravity investigations are useful in

1. Exploration of ore deposits
2. In exploration of Oil and natural gas deposits
3. In solving regional geological problems
4. In case of engineering problems like mapping of dams sites, earthquake problems etc

## *Name the types of classifiers on the basis of separation?*

1. Wet classifiers
2. Dry classifiers

## *How many types of classification in industrial classifiers? Name them.*

Three

1. Hydraulic classifiers
2. Mechanical classifiers
3. Cyclones classifiers

## *On which things velocity of particles in fluid depends?*

- Size
- Specific gravity
- Shape of particles

### *What is air classification?*

- It is a process of separating categories of materials by way of differences in the respective aerodynamic characteristics.

### *Name three types of wet classifiers.*

1. Gravity settling tank
2. Cone classifier
3. Sprial classifier

### *Differentiate between CSTR and PFR.*

1. In CSTR there is wide range of residence time of molecules while in PFR all molecules spend equal time in reactor.
2. There is complete mixing in CSTR while in PFR there is only radial mixing but no axial mixing.
3. Less conversion in CSTR while more conversion in PFR.

### *How could use increase productivity of CSTRs?*

- By connecting several CSTRs in series, such that product of one CSTR is reactant of other.

### *How residence time distribution in measured for reactors?*

- The RTD is determined experimentally by injecting an inert chemical, molecule, or atom, called a tracer, into the reactor at some time t =0 and then measuring the tracer concentration, C, in the effluent stream as a function of time.

### *What is heat transfer?*

- It is a result of the $2^{nd}$ law of thermodynamics which states that heat will flow from high to low temperature until equal temperature are obtained.

### *What are main heat transfer mechanism?*

- Conduction
- Convection
- Radiation

## *What is conduction?*

- Thermal conduction is the transfer of internal energy by microscopic collisions of particles and movement of electrons within a body. The colliding particles, which include molecules, atoms and electrons, transfer disorganized microscopic kinetic and potential energy, jointly known as internal energy. Conduction takes place in all phases: solid, liquid, and gas. The rate at which energy is conducted as heat between two bodies depends on the temperature difference (and hence temperature gradient) between the two bodies and the properties of the conductive interface through which the heat is transferred.

## *What is Convection?*

- Convection is the heat transfer due to the bulk movement of molecules within fluids such as gases and liquids, including molten rock (rheid). Convection includes sub-mechanisms of advection (directional bulk-flow transfer of heat), and diffusion (non-directional transfer of energy or mass particles along a concentration gradient).

## *What is radiation?*

- Radiation is a method of heat transfer that does not rely upon any contact between the heat source and the heated object as is the case with conduction and convection. Heat can be transmitted through empty space by thermal radiation often called infrared radiation. This is a type electromagnetic radiation. No mass is exchanged and no medium is required in the process of radiation.

## *Why heat transfer is importance in rectors?*

- Because there is loss of heat through walls of reactor to surrounding atmosphere due to which temperature drop inside reactor but we have to maintain a temperature... So we have to calculate losses via different heat transfer mechanism to maintain temperature.

## *What are some inherently safer design?*

1. Use large number of small reactors (process miniaturization)
2. Use more active catalyst

### *What is jigging?*

- Jigging is a density-separation process which is widely used to separate heavier particles from the lighter ones.

### *Where is jigging mainly used?*

- It is used for beneficiation of ore minerals as well as washing of coal.

### *What is the necessary condition for jigging ?*

- The condition necessary for the correct separation of particles in a separating device, a jig, is sufficient loosening of the feed particles in a working bed.

### *What is the optimum pulse rate for stratification?*

- Particles were best separated when they were operated at or near the natural frequency of the lighter material.

### *How does air flow rates affect the stratification process?*

- The separation rate increases first with increasing air flow rate and decreases after reaching a maximum value.

### *How is the motion of a conventional jig?*

- The motion of a conventional jig is harmonic. The two phases are pulsation and suction.

### *What basic change is made in the conventional jig to modify it into IHC jig drive?*

- The harmonic motion of the conventional eccentric-driven jig is replaced by an asymmetrical 'saw tooth' movement of the diaphragm with a rapid upward followed by a slow downward stroke.

### *What is the main difference between distillation and solvent extraction? when is the solvent extraction preferred over distillation?*

- Distillation follows heating of a liquid mixture and collecting the vapour of liquid at their boiling pt but solvent extraction doesn't requires heating.
- For sensitive components like antibodies, vitamins and recovery of solute from very dilute solution solvent extraction is used over distillation.

## *How is extraction efficiency denoted for practical purpose?*

- Extraction efficiency is denoted by percent extraction.

%extraction= 100D/D+(v aqueous/ v organic)
Where, D is distribution ratio
And v is the volume

## *Why is aluminium not used for precipitation despite having greater oxidation potential than zinc?*

- The protective oxide layer formed on the aluminium surface during oxidation makes it unsuitable for precipitation process.

## *Why is the extraction of cobalt and nickel not favourable by solvent extraction in zinc purification?*

- Zinc gets coextracted along with these metals which makes their extraction process non-beneficial.

## *Define 'roasting'?*

- Roasting is the process of converting sulphide ores to oxides by heating the ores in a regular supply of air at a temperature below the melting point of the metal.For example,sulphide ores of Zn,Pb and Cu are converted to their respective oxides by this process.

## *How is copper extracted from low grade copper ores?*

- The low-grade copper ore contains 0.27% Cu, in which the major copper-bearing mineral is chalcopyrite associated with other minerals present as minor phase. The low-grade copper ore procured from Malanjkhand, Madhya Pradesh, India was used as leaching material.
- Copper can be obtained from low grade ore through the process of leaching using acid or bacteria (leaching is a process in which ore is treated with suitable reagent which dissolves ore but not the impurities).
- Now the copper goes through reduction process. As copper as lower reactivity than hydrogen so it is reduced using hydrogen.

## *Write two basic requirements for refining of a metal by Mond process .*

The two basic requirements for Mond's process are:

1. The metal should form a volatile compound with an available reagent,
2. The volatile compound should be easily decomposable, so that the recovery is easy

## *How do we separate two sulphide ores by Froth Floatation Method? Explain with an example*

- In the froth floatation, the role of depressants is to separate two sulphide ores by selectively preventing one ore from forming froth. For example, to separate two sulphide ores (ZnS and PbS) , NaCN is used as a depressant which selectively allows PbS to come with froth ,but prevents ZnS from coming to froth. This happens because NaCN reacts with ZnS to form $Na_2[Zn(CN)_4]$.

$$4\ NaCN + ZnS \text{ GIVES } Na_2[Zn(CN)_4] + Na_2S$$

## *What should be the considerations during the extraction of metals by electrochemical method?*

- In the electrochemical method for the extraction of metals, the following considerations are significant.

1. The reactivity of the metal which is produced. For example, if sodium is isolated by this method, it immediately reacts with water violently. This problem does not arise in case of metal like copper.
2. The choice of the electrodes is of great significance. For example, when aqueous solution of $CuSO_4$ is electrolyed using inert electrodes (e.g. Pt-electrodes), the products formed are different than in case when attackable electrodes are used.

## *What is difference between electro-refining and carbonyl refining?*

- In electrorefining, the nickel is deposited onto pure nickel cathodes from sulfate or chloride solutions.
- In carbonyl refining, carbon monoxide is passed through the matte, yielding nickel and iron carbonyls [$Ni(CO)_4$ and $Fe(CO)_5$]

## *Why is the reduction of a metal oxide is easier if the metal formed is in liquid state at the temperature of reduction?*

- The reduction of a metal oxide is easier because entropy increases in liquid state.

### *At a site low grade copper ores are available and zinc and iron scraps are also available. Which of the two scraps would be more suitable for reducing the leached copper ore and why?*

- Zinc is a costlier metal than iron, so using iron scraps will be advisable and advantageous

### *On what basis are roll crushers classified ?*

- On the basis of Weather the rollers are toothed or not and on the basis of number of cylinders

### *Types of rod mills ?*

- Central peripheral discharge, End peripheral discharge and Trunnion overflow mills

### *Types of auto-genous mills ?*

- Vibratory, Centrifugal, Tower, Stirred and Roller mill

### *What does hinder settling and free settling classifiers effects on separation?*

- Hinder settling classfiers increases effect of density and free settling classifiers increases effect of size on seperation

### *Explain different types of distillation?*

- Simple distillation: process of converting a liquid into its vapours which are passed through a cooling surface to condense its vapors.

1. **Flash distillation:** a process in which entire liquid mixture is suddenly vaporized by passing the feed through a high pressure zone to low pressure zone.
2. **Fractional distillation:** process in which vaporization of liquid mixtures give rise to mixture of constituents from which the desired ore is separated in pure form.
3. **Azotropic distillation:** process in which azotropic mixture is broken by addition of a third substance
4. **Extractive distillation:** same as azotropic distillation except the fact that the third agent is non volatile.
5. **Distillation under reduced pressure:** A distillation process in which liquid is distilled at a temperature lower than its boiling point by the application of vaccum.
6. **Steam distillation:** method of distillation carried out with a aid of steam and is used for separation of high boiling substances from non volatile impurities.

7. **Molecular distillation**: distillation process in which each molecule in the vapour phase travels mean free path and gets condensed individually without intermolecular collisions.
8. **Destructive distillation:** a process in which the distillate is decomposition product of the constituents of the organic matter burnt in the absence of air.
9. **Compression distillation:** developed to meet the needs of navy and army for fresh water which is obtained from sea water.

### *Differentiate between simple distillation and fractional distillation ?*

- The main difference between fractional distillation and simple distillation is that simple distillation separate liquids with boiling point gaps of at least 50 degrees whereas fractional distillation separates liquids with closer boiling points.

### *What is refining?*

- The process of removing impurities from metals is called refining.

### *What is distillation?*

- It is a process of separating one component of a liquid mixture according to difference in boiling point.

### *What is Fire refining?*

- It is a method to remove more reactive elements from a molten metal by preferential oxidation.

### *How is the Oxygen supplied in Fire refining?*

- Oxygen can be supplied directly through air or indirectly through salts such as Sodium Nitrate as it is an Oxidising agent which decomposes to give nascent Oxygen.

### *What are metallurgical fuels? Give some examples?*

- Fuels which are physical and chemical characteristics for economic metals production are known as Metallurgical Fuels. Examples: Cooking Coals, Metallurgical Coke , Fuels for different blast furnaces.

### *What do you mean by calorific value? How it is calculated?*

- Calorific Value of a fuel is the quantity of heat produced by its consumption at constant pressure and at normal conditions.
- The carolific value is calculated by using heat balance i.e. Heat given by the fuel is equal to the heat gained by the water.

### *What are the different properties of charcoal?*

The main properties are:-

1. Low ash generation
2. High combustibility
3. High reactivity with CO2
4. Low mechanical strength
5. High moisture absorption

### *What are the different types of coking coal?*

There are three types of coking coal:-

1. Hard Coking Coal
2. Semi Soft Coking Coal
3. Pulverized Coal Injection

### *What are the types of coal on the basis of calorific Value?*

There are four types of coal on the basis of calorifi value:-

1. Anthracite - 30 MJ/Kg
2. Bituminous - 18.8-29.3 MJ/Kg
3. Sub Bituminous - 8.3-25 MJ/Kg
4. Lignite - 5.5-14.3 MJ/Kg

### *What is the key requirements of producing biomass?*

The requirements are:-

1. Low ash content.
2. Sulfur content between .01-.05%.
3. High reactivity with CO2 about .3- 3 g/s2

### *Why coke and coal is directly used as a fuel ?*

- The properties of coal and coke are very suitable for characteristics of fuels i.e. generates intense heat with low amount of smoke.

### *What are the main categories of metallurgical coals?*

The main categories of metallurgical coals are as follows:

1. Hard coking coals (HCC)
2. Semi-soft coking coal (SSCC)
3. Pulverized coal injection (PCI) coal

### *How can biomass derived materials be utilised?*

- Biomass growing and absorbing CO2 from atmosphere
- Harvesting and utilisation for combustion
- Recycling of carbon dioxide back into the storage

### *What are the main properties of metallurgical coke?*

The main functions are:-

1. Energy for the endothermic chemical reaction.
2. Reducing gases to convert iron oxides to metallic iron.
3. Mechanical support for the burden.

### *What are the properties which give rise to the manufacture of coke?*

The properties are:-

- Carbon contain of 85-88%
- Hydrogen should vary from 3.7-4.5%.
- Sulfur both organic and inorganic should not exceed .75%.
- Phosphorous lies between .15-.25%.

### *Describe a electric arc furnace?*

- An electric arc furnace is a furnace in which heat is charged to the material by means of an electric arc. This greatly reduces the energy required to form steel.

### *Describe electric induction furnace*

- In induction furnace a coil carrying alternate varying current surrounds the container and chamber of the metal. The Eddy current induced in the metal and the circulation of this current produce heat enough to melt the metal and produce alloys of exact composition.

### *What is the advantage of induction heating in electric induction furnace?*

- Advantage of induction heating is that heat is generated within the furnace charge itself rather than being applied by a burning fuel or any other external agencies.

### *What are the modern fuels used for different metallurgical processes?*

1. Biomass is used for steel making.
2. Natural gas is used in Open Hearth Process.
3. Hydrogen is used in production of stainless steel alloy.
4. Electricity is used in Electric Arc Furnace.
5. Technical Hydrolysis Lignin is used in BOF process.

### *How are reducing agents prepared?*

- The plastic waste collected enter a treating process and the material mix is specified and finally pelletized to be used as a reducing agent.

### *How are direct refuced iron produced?*

- DRC are produced by direct reduction of iron ore to iron by reducing gas or elemental carbon from natural gas or coal.

### *What is THL?*

- THL is a waste product formed in paper and pulp industries due to the cemical treatment of wood biomass and substandard agricultural raw materials.

### *Which type of fuels come under metallurgical fuels?*

- Coking coals
- Metallurgical coke
- Fuels fir injection to blast furnace to produce iron for steel making

### *What is "Equivalent Diameter"?*

- The diameter of a sphere that would behave in the same manner as the particle when submitted to some specified operation.

### *Explain "Seive Analysis"?*

- Sieve analysis is one of the oldest methods of size analysis and is accomplished by passing a known weight of sample material successively through finer sieves and weighing the amount collected on each sieve to determine the percentage weight in each size fraction. Sieving is carried out with wet or dry materials and the sieves are usually agitated to expose all the particles to the openings.

### *What is the Significance of Particle Size Distribution?*

- PSD can be important in understanding physical and chemical properties of material.
- It affects the strength and load bearing properties of rocks and soils.
- It affects the reactivity of solid participating in chemical reaction and gives control over it.

### *What are the factors on which "Effectiveness" of seive test depends?*

- The effectiveness of a sieving test depends on the amount of material put on the sieve (the "charge") and the type of movement imparted to the sieve

### *Define "Charge" and "mesh number"?*

- Charge isamount of material put on the sieve .
- Mesh number is referred to the number of square apertures per square inch.

### *What are Disadvantages of "Seive analysis test" ?*

- Particle size less than 100 microns cannot be distributed with this method.
- Particles after seive test is fragile and sometimes in the form of elongated needlles.
- The material adheres to the seive or form clumps and powder can easily aquire electrostatic charge

## *What are " Subseive range" and " name the process carried out for seperation of these particles" ?*

- Below 38 micron; below this size the operation is referred to as sub-sieving. The most widely used methods are sedimentation, elutriation, microscopy, and laser diffraction

## *Explain Sedemetation?*

- Sedimentation methods are based on the measurement of the rate of settling of the powder particles uniformly dispersed in a fluid. In sedimentation techniques, the material to be sized is dispersed in a fluid and allowed to settle under carefully controlled conditions;

## *What are advantages of sedimentation process?*

- This method is simple and cheap and have advatage over other sub-seive techniques in that it produces true fractional size analysis

## *What is disadvantage of sedimetation method?*

- Method is extremely tedious, long settling time is required for very fine particles and seperate test must be performed for each size particles.

## *Why we have need of alternative reductants?*

- Limited amount of coal in nature and to reduce the pollution by coke and coal.

## *Write the some name of alternative reductants?*

- Shredder residue material (srm)., charcoal from agriculture residue, Hydrogen, hydrogen plasma, waste polyethylene terephthlate.

## *Alternative reducing agent by which not occur pollution?*

- Hydrogen & Hydrogen plasma

## *Why hydrogen plasma is economically more feasible reductants?*

- Due to ellimination of multiple process like Palletisation, coke making & sintering and other reason release of some energy at reduction interface by Hydrogen species.

## *What is Heterogeneous catalysis ?*

- Heterogeneous catalysis is the type of catalysis where the phase of the catalyst differs from the phase of the reactants or products.

## *How many types of heterogenous catalysts is there ?*

Two types-

1. Reactors with insignificant motion of catalyst particles
2. Reactors with significant motion of catalyst particles

## *Mention the all the types of Reactors with insignificant motion of catalyst particles*

- They are mainly four types-

1. Fixed bed reactor,
2. Trickle-bed reactor
3. Moving bed reactor,
4. Rotating bed reactor

## *Mention the types of Reactors with significant motion of catalyst particles*

- Two types-

1. Fluidized bed reactors
2. Slurry reactors

### *what is fixed bed reactor ?*

- A fixed bed reactor is a cylindrical tube filled with catalyst pellets with reactants flowing through the bed and being converted into products.

### *Describes at least one application of fixed bed reactor.*

- Synthesis of valuable chemicals

### *Describe all the types of design procedures that have been used.*

1. Isothermal operation
2. Adiabatic operation
3. Non-adiabatic operation
4. Non-isothermal operation
5. Simplified method 6-Semi-rigorous procedure

### *Mention the two types of mechanism that used in fixed bed reactor.*

1. Mass transfer
2. Heat transfer

### *Why high temperature is required in reduction process of iron ore?*

- Carbon can reduce any metal oxide and lower oxides (CO) are more stable than metal oxides at high temperature.

### *What is the difference between coal-based and gas-based reduction?*

- Natural gases are used as reducing agent in gas-based reduction while in coal-based reduction coking coal are used as a solid reducing agent.

### *Why direct reduction process is used over conventional blast furnaces?*

- It is more energy sufficient and operating cost is low and it is good for the countries where availability of coal is low.

### *Why Methane reforming and water shift reaction is also important in reduction of iron?*

- It increases the rate of reduction and continuous regeneration of reducing agent (CO & H2) occurs.

### *How does a vibrating screen work?*

- A vibrating mechanism attached to the middle of the screen imparts rapid vibrations of small amplitude to its surface, making the ore, which enters at the top, pass down it in an even mobile stream.

### *Why should oxygen be removed before cementation of Zn-Cu solution takes place?*

- At low ph values, the cementing metal reacts with hydrogen and oxygen ions and therefore they should be removed beforehand.

### *What is azeotropic mixture?*

- Mixture containing two or more components whose proportion cannot be altered by simple distillation.

### *What precaution must be taken during distillation?*

- Proper ventilation should always be ensured because alcohol diffuses with air and can cause explosion.

### *What is double distillation used for?*

- It is used for carrying out reactions under stirred conditions along with furnishing of reflux distillation.

### *Copper can be extracted by hydrometallurgy but not zinc. Explain*

- Because the order of reducing power of zinc , copper and water is as follows:-. Zn>water>Cu

### *What is the objective of mixing and agitation?*

1. To increase the homogeneity of material on bulk.
2. To bring about intimate contact between different species in order for a chemical reaction to occur.
3. To change the texture
4. To enhance heat and mass transfer
5. To dispense a liquid which is immiscible with the other liquid by forming an emulsion or suspension of few drops.

## *Fill in the blanks :*

- The volume of the ore slurry is determined by ___1___ amount and ___2___ concentration grade.

1. Dry ore
2. Feed ore

## *What is Flotation in Mineral Processing?*

- Froth flotation is a process for selectively separating hydrophobic materials from hydrophilic. This is used in mineral processing, paper recycling and waste-water treatment industries.

## *What is the Principle of Froth Flotation process?*

- Flotation uses the manipulation of surface chemistry to preferentially upgrade valuable minerals into a concentrate. The particles that are frothed become lighter and they float at the top of the container.

## *What is a Flotation Machine?*

- Flotation Machines constitute the basic equipment for useful mineral recovery from non-ferrous ores and other raw materials by flotation.

## *What are the requirements of a good Flotation Machine?*

- Good mixing of pulp
- Appropriate aeration and dispersion of fine gas bubbles
- Sufficient control of pulp agitation in the froth zone
- Efficient mass flow mechanisms.

## *What are the factors affecting the selection of a particular flotation machine?*

1. Metallurgical Performance
2. Ease of operation
3. Cost
4. Capacity

### *What are the types of flotation machines?*

1. Mechanical
2. Pneumatic
3. Dissolved air flotation

### *What are Mechanical Flotation Machines?*

- A Mechanical machine consists of a mechanically driven impeller that disperses air into the agitated pulp.

### *What are the types of Mechanical flotation machine?*

1. Self-Aeration
2. Supercharged

### *What are the uses of agitation and aeration?*

- Aeration - Increases Chances of Particle Contact
- Agitation - Maintains particles in suspension.

### *What are Flotation Columns?*

- This machine provides a counter-current flow of air bubbles and slurry with a long contact time and plenty of wash water.These generates high separation grade

### *What is the Heat of reaction?*

- The Heat of Reaction is the change in the enthalpy of a chemical reaction that occurs at a constant pressure.

## *What are the materials used in making heat exchangers?*

- Ceramics are a particularly good choice for the kind of high-temperature applications (over 1000°C or 2000°F) that would melt metals like copper, iron, and steel. Some metals, composites and polymers are also used. currently, research on using carbon nanotubes as a material of the heat exchanger is being done due to its amazing heat conducting properties

## *What is Reynolds number?*

- The Reynolds number is the ratio of inertial forces to viscous forces within a fluid which is subjected to relative internal movement due to different fluid velocities.

## *What is viscosity?*

- The viscosity of a fluid is a measure of its resistance to deformation at a given rate.

## *What is cold fuel gas?*

- A cold gas thruster uses the expansion of a (typically inert) pressurized gas to generate thrust.

## *Where is adiabatic reactor used?*

- Adiabatic reactor finds application in catalyst testing when final product quality must be evaluated and the reacting system has a high heat release.

## *Why is solid liquid mixing carried out at batch operation?*

- In order to allow more accurate control of dissolved solid concentration, mixing of solids and liquids is often carried out as a batch operation

## *How do we calculate residence time?*

- The residence time defined for steady-state systems is equal to the reservoir volume divided by the inflow or outflow rate

### *Define primary crusher.*

- Primary crushers are heavy duty machines used to reduced run- of mine ore down to size suitable for transport and for feeding the secondary crusher.

### *How many types of primary crusher? Name them.*

- Two types

1. Jaw crusher
2. Gyratory crusher

### *What type of structure jaw crusher have?*

- It has two plate one is fixed and other one is swings relative to the fixed plate. Angle between these plates is acute.

### *What are the main feature of jaw crusher?*

- Simple structure hence easy maintenance
- Stable performance
- High crushing ratio

### *On the basis of method of pivoting the swing jaw how many type of jaw crusher ? Name them.*

- Three type

1. Blake crusher
2. Dodge crusher
3. Universal crusher

### *What are the main difference between Dodge, Blake, Universal crusher on the basis of the their structure?*

1. Blake- in Blake crusher jaw is pivoted at the top hence it has fixed receiving area and variable discharge opening.
2. Dodge - in dodge crusher jaw is pivoted at the bottom, so that it has variable receiving area and fixed discharge opening.

3. Universal - here jaw is pivoted intermediate between top and bottom of plate. So that it has variable receiving area and discharge opening.

### *Define gyratory crusher on the basis of the their stucfure.*

- Gyratory crusher include a solid cone set on a revolving shaft placed with in a hollow body which has conical or vertical slopping sides.

### *What is grinding ?*

- Ans: Grinding is accomplished by impact of attrition and abrasion of the ore by free motion of unconnected media . It usually performed wet to produce slurry feed on concentration process. It is greatest energy consumer process and it takes upto 50% of total energy consumption.

### *HPGR is new technology. For what purpose this technology is made.*

- It is made by taking care of energy consumption. It is 20-50% more efficient than conventional crusher and mill. It is usually used in cement factory.

### *What is reduction ratio of crushing stage?*

- Mathematically it is defined as-

  Reduction ratio = (maximum size of particle enter the crusher) / (minimum size of particle leave the crusher).

### *What is fluidization?*

- A fluid (gas or liquid) is passed through a solid granular material at high enough velocities to suspend the solid and cause it to behave as though it were a fluid. This process, known as fluidization

### *What is FBR?*

- A fluidized bed reactor (FBR) is a type of reactor device that can be used to carry out a variety of multiphase chemical reactions.

## *Explain the basic principles involved in a FBR*

- The solid substrate (the catalytic material upon which chemical species react) material in the fluidized bed reactor is typically supported by a porous plate, known as a distributor. The fluid is then forced through the distributor up through the solid material. As the fluid velocity is increased, the reactor will reach a stage where the force of the fluid on the solids is enough to balance the weight of the solid material. This stage is known as incipient fluidization and occurs at this minimum fluidization velocity. Once this minimum velocity is surpassed, the contents of the reactor bed begin to expand and swirl around much like an agitated tank or boiling pot of water.

## *What is minimum fluidization velocity?*

- As the fluid velocity is increased, the reactor will reach a stage where the force of the fluid on the solids is enough to balance the weight of the solid material. This stage is known as incipient fluidization and occurs at this minimum fluidization velocity.

## *What are advantages of a FBR?*

1. Uniform Particle Mixing: Due to the intrinsic fluid-like behavior of the solid material, fluidized beds do not experience poor mixing as in packed beds. This complete mixing allows for a uniform product that can often be hard to achieve in other reactor designs.
2. Uniform Temperature Gradients: Many chemical reactions require the addition or removal of heat. Local hot or cold spots within the reaction bed, often a problem in packed beds, are avoided in a fluidized situation such as an FBR.
3. Ability to Operate Reactor in Continuous State: The fluidized bed nature of these reactors allows for the ability to continuously withdraw product and introduce new reactants into the reaction vessel.

## *What are disadvantages of a FBR*

1. Increased Reactor Vessel Size: Because of the expansion of the bed materials in the reactor, a larger vessel is often required than that for a packed bed reactor.
2. Lack of Current Understanding: Current understanding of the actual behavior of the materials in a fluidized bed is rather limited. It is very difficult to predict and calculate the complex mass and heat flows within the bed.
3. Erosion of Internal Components: The fluid-like behavior of the fine solid particles within the bed eventually results in the wear of the reactor vessel and hence increases cost.
4. Pressure Loss Scenarios: If fluidization pressure is suddenly lost, the surface area of the bed may be suddenly reduced. This can either be an inconvenience (e.g. making bed restart difficult), or may have more serious implications, such as runaway reactions.

## *Explain current research and trends on a FBR*

- Most current research aims to quantify and explain the behavior of the phase interactions in the bed. Specific research topics include particle size distributions, various transfer coefficients, phase interactions, velocity and pressure effects, and computer modeling. The aim of this research is to produce more accurate models of the inner movements and phenomena of the bed. This will enable chemical engineers to design better, more efficient reactors that may effectively deal with the current disadvantages of the technology and expand the range of FBR use.

## *What is the role of Calcination in metallurgy operation?*

- To remove moisture
- To decompose carbonate
- To drive off organic matters

## *What are the factors on which the magnetic force on a particle in a magnetic separator depends?*

- Magnetic susceptibility of the particle, the fluid medium, applied magnetic field and magnetic field gradient

## *How does grade recovery is utilised?*

- Utilized to identify potential recovery quickly and it can help to optimize the flotation process which can be more efficient.

## *What materials are required for tabling?*

- A shaking table and water
- Three 100 g samples (25% ilmenite and 75%silica)
- Magnetic separator

## *If we increase the grade what will happen to recovery rate?*

- Grade and recovery are generally inversely proportion also if we increase the grade automatically rate of reduction gets decreases.

## *What is the first step in mineral processing?*

- The first step in mineral processing which takes place at the Mining site is. Smelting. The process of heating an ore Beyond its melting point and combining it with others substances is called.

## *what changes did you observed while conducting experiments at 30Hz and 37Hz?*

- Recovery is relatively high, therefore it is expected that the grade be lower compared to when the frequency was set at 30 Hz. However, the grades are about the same i.e 28%.whereas in 30Hz recovery is 58%.

## *What is the major role played in frequency table?*

- Experiment carried out at the 40 Hz frequency was the most effective as it produced a higher grade separation in a relatively short amount of time.

## *What will be if heavier metal used in frequency table. Give your observation?*

- Minerals that were the heaviest separated slower than the lighter and finer particles, which were carried by the water easier and rolled on the surface of the table instead of sliding.

## *What are flocculants?*

- Polymers carrying cationic or anionic charge that bind tiny particles together to build much larger particles

## *Metal with more negative electropotential displaces the metal with less negative potential.*

- Metal with more negative electropotential displaces the metal with less negative potential.

## *What do you mean by sintering?*

- It is the process of compacting and forming a solid mass of materia by heat or pressure without melting it to the point of liquefaction.

## *Define pulverization.*

- Pulverization is a process of crushing solid material into a fine particles of less than 5 mm.

### *Which is better for reduction of niobium. Calcium/Magnesium...and why?*

- Magnesium is better because it has a high vapour pressure even at a moderate boiling temp of 1363k.

### *What do you mean by calcination?*

- Heating a substance in the absence or limited supply of air or oxygen.

### *What do you mean by metallothermic reduction?*

- Reduction of compunds using a metal such as aluminium or silicon as the reducing agent is called a metallothermic reduction...

### *What are the various process stages involved in hydrometallurgy?*

- The various processes involved in hydrometallurgy are:

1. Leaching ,
2. Solution concentration and purification ,
3. Metal recovery

### *Why is ore size reduced while leaching?*

- The ore size is reduced through crushing and grinding while leaching so that the surface area of particles increases and, therefore, the reaction rate.

### *State any two factors leading to choice of leachant.*

- The factors are:

1. Chemical and physical character of the material to be leached.
2. Cost of the reagent.

### *Name the common categories of leaching reagents.With example.*

- The common leaching reagents are :

1. Water
2. Acids – $H_2SO_4$ , $HNO_3$
3. Bases – NaOH , $NH_4OH$
4. Aqueous salt solutions – NaCN solution

### *State an advantage of heap leaching .*

- A major advantage of heap leaching is the elimination of expensive milling operations since the ore body need not be crushed to sizes much smaller than 20 to 25 mm.

### *What's the need to melt the ore in smelting process?*

- The smelting process melts the ore, usually for a chemical change to separate the metal, thereby reducing or refining it.

### *What are the parameters used during Smelting?*

- Use the applications of heat, leaching in a strong acidic or alkaline solution, or electrolytic processes.

### *Why steel qualities varies during the smelting process?*

- During smelting, the removal degrees of impurities by different smelting methods are not the same, so the steel qualities are different.

### *How many types of steels are produced by Smelting process?*

- Recently, there are three kinds of steel, including Bessemer steel (converter steel), Siemens-Martin steel, and electric steel.

### *What's the role of reducing reagents (like carbon) in Smelting process?*

- The Carbon removes the oxygen from the ore and leaves the elemental metal. Carbon oxidises in two stages 1$^{st}$ is carbon monoxide and the other is carbon dioxide to remove the slag from impure ores.

## *What happens in Corex process?*

- Corex process conceived as a means of producing iron in face of increasing gas prices and reducing coking coal resources.
- 1[st] of all coal is fed into the melter gasifier which operates under pressure and the upper region of the reactor being at temperature of 1000-1200°C results in rapid drying and degasification of the coal. In this process carbon oxidises to carbon dioxide then reacts with free carbon accordingly to form Carbon monoxide. The reducing gas after cleaning from dust particles is fed into the reduction shaft furnance where reduction occurs .Further in the gasifier, the metallisation rates are in the order of 95% where sponge iron is continuously fed with the temperature between 800-900°C along with 3-6% of carbon contents in it results into final reduction and melting occurs.

## *What are the limitations of Corex process?*

- It uses fine ores.
- High silica and aluminium ores create problem in reduction shaft.
- So it was essential to clean dust from the melter gasifier before passing into the reduction shaft.

## *What are the drawbacks of the Smelting process?*

- Toxic Air Pollutants
- Water Pollution
- Acid Rain
- Workers at smelting plants are exposed to toxic chemicals every day. Although the environmental damage done can be costly to the public.

## *Which component occurs due to mixing that acting on the liquid?*

1. Radial component
2. Tangential/circular component
3. Axial/longitudinal component

## *What is the basic difference between smelting and melting?*

- Both processes involve heat, but melting is a simple phase change: the substance changes from a solid to a liquid but its identity doesn't change. The smelting process, however, uses heat to produce a chemical change.

### *Why is smelting done above melting point?*

- For smelting metal's, it is done at a very high temperature above their melting point to either reduce or oxidize the metal resulting in to form a shape for further use. This is done in a furnace of very high temperature which powers the reaction of combustion along with red-ox reactions.

### *What is slag?*

- Slag is the glass-like by-product left over after a desired metal has been separated (i.e., smelted) from its raw ore.

### *What are the two types into which slags can be broadly classified?*

- Slags can be broadly classified as :

1. Iron and Steel Slags
2. Non Ferrous Slags

### *What is comminution?*

- It is particle size reduction of materials. It may be carried out on either dry materials or slurries.

### *What are the two types into which Iron and Steel slags can be classified?*

- The Iron and Steel Slags are again classified into :

1. Blast Furnace slag
2. Steel making slag

### *What is Blast Furnace Slag?*

- Blast furnace slag is recovered by melting separation from blast furnaces that produce molten pig iron. It consists of non-ferrous components contained in the iron ore together with limestone as an auxiliary materials and ash from coke.

### *What are the primary components present in a steel slag?*

- The primary components of blast furnace slag are limestone (CaO) and silica ($SiO_2$). Other components include alumina ($Al_2O_3$) and magnesium oxide (MgO), as well as a small amount of sulfur (S)

## *What are the types into which blast furnace slags can be classified based on their cooling method?*

- Depending on the cooling method used, the blast furnace slag is classified:

1. Air-cooled slag
2. Granulated slag

## *What is Air-Cooled Slag?*

- The molten slag flows into a cooling yard, where it is cooled slowly by natural cooling and by spraying with water. This results in a crystalline, rock-like air-cooled slag.

## *What is Granulated Slag?*

- The molten slag is cooled rapidly by jets of pressurized water, resulting in a vitreous, granulated slag.

## *What is the application of Air-cooled slag?*

The applications of air-cooled slags are:

- 1. Road base course material
- 2. Coarse aggregate for concrete
- 3. Cement clinker raw material (replacement for clay)
- 4. Raw material for rock wool
- 5. Calcium silicate fertilizer

## *What are the two types of Steel making slag?*

- Steelmaking slag consists of two types:
- Converter slag
- Electric arc furnace slag

## *Amygdaloidal structures have of*

- 1)The vesicles of the volcanic rock may subsequently be filled by the secondary minerals
- 2)such as calcite and zeolite
- 3)filled vesicles called amygdales

## *How is the Ellingham diagram helpful in the metallurgical process?*

- In Ellingham diagram elements present below in the diagram reduce elements above in the diagram. thus it helps in the selection of suitable reducing agents as well as optimum temperature.

## *What are the Costs of Geophysics?*

- The application of geophysics must be assessed in terms of its projected costs and benefits. It makes no sense to conduct a geophysical survey if the costs are projected to exceed any possible economic gains, or to exceed the project's operational budget. In general, however,geophysical surveys are almost always substantially less expensive than traditional nontechnical means of investigation such as excavation or drilling.

## *Crushing and grinding are two comminution process. Explain how they are carried out?*

- Crushing normally carried out on run of mine ore. Grinding carried out after crushing. May be conducted on dry or slurried material.

## *What are the forces involved in size reduction?*

- Compression, impact, attrition

## *Difference between primary and secondary crusher?*

- Primary crusher is only for breaking of large stones into pieces. That is not for aggregate size material. After that secondary crusher comes into action and further reduces in size.

## *What are different types of internal grinding machine?*

- Chuking, planetary, centerless.

### *What are mineral sizers?*

- A variety of roll crusher which use 2 rotors with large teeth on small diameter shafts, driven at a low speed by direct high torque driven system.

### *What are the principles of minerals sizer?*

- Breaking action, rotating screen effect, and deep scroll tooth pattern.

### *What is screening?*

- screening is to separate from a granular substance particle that are smaller than the screen opening from those that are larger.

### *What are the size limitations of Dry screening and Wet screening?*

- Dry screening is generally limited to the material above about 5 mm in size, while wet screening is down to around 250μm.

### *What is a micron?*

- Micron is the measure of length most frequently used to describe tiny particle sizes. The term micron is actually a commonly used shorthand for micrometre. The official symbol for the micron or micrometre is μm. A micron is defined as one-millionth of a meter, a little more than one twenty-five thousandth of an inch.

### *What is mesh?*

- A mesh is a barrier made of connected strands of metal, fiber, or other flexible or ductile materials. A mesh is similar to a web or a net in that it has many attached or woven strands.

### *What is most common in glassy silicic rocks that have interacted with water to become hydrated*

- Perlite

### *The process by which rock is broken down as a result of a chemical reaction:*

- Chemical weathering

### *What are the main objectives of screening?*

- (a)Sizing or Classifying
- (b) Scalping
- (c) Grading
- (d) Media recovery
- (e) Dewatering
- (f)Desliming or de-dusting
- (g)Trash removal

### *What are the factors affecting the screen Performance?*

- (a)Particle size
- (b) Feed rate
- (c) Screen angle
- (d) Particle shape
- (e) Open area
- (f)Vibration
- (g)Moisture

### *What is comminution?*

- It is particle size reduction of materials. It may be carried out on either dry materials or slurries.

### *Upto what range materials can be feed into jaw crusher?*

- 125mm- 1500mm.

### *Difference between jaw and cone crusher?*

- Cone crusher is secondary crusher. It can feed materials upto 35mm- 350mm. Jaw crusher is primary crusher and can feed material up to 125mm- 1500mm.

Printed by Libri Plureos GmbH in Hamburg,
Germany